Gien Karssen is a storyteller. Although there are many studies about the women in the Bible, I have never read one more practical than *Her Name Is Woman*. Gien makes these biblical women really come alive as you observe their actions and the effects of their lives. She helps you draw out applications that are relevant today. Gien is one of the best trainers I know for young Bible study leaders. She brings the Word of God to bear upon situations in day-to-day living. My prayer is that this book will work as a seed that brings forth much fruit.

CORRIE TEN BOOM
Author of *The Hiding Place*

All my life I have read about the women of the Bible, learning much from them even though they were somewhat vague, historic characters. In this book, these same characters have suddenly come alive. Because of Gien's careful research, sanctified imagination, and skill as a writer, I found myself understanding these women and their situations in a new way. Knowing more about the customs of their day helps us understand better why they acted as they did. It is interesting to note that God's women, down through the centuries, have enjoyed a freedom the world finds difficult to understand— the freedom to be and to do that which God intended. You will find this book both interesting and enlightening.

RUTH BELL GRAHAM
Author of *Footprints of a Pilgrim*

Wanderers

lessons from women of stubborn hearts

HER NAME IS WOMAN BIBLE STUDY

Gien Karssen

A NavPress resource published in alliance
with Tyndale House Publishers, Inc.

NAVPRESS⬤®

NavPress is the publishing ministry of The Navigators, an international Christian organization and leader in personal spiritual development. NavPress is committed to helping people grow spiritually and enjoy lives of meaning and hope through personal and group resources that are biblically rooted, culturally relevant, and highly practical.

For more information, visit www.NavPress.com.

Wanderers: Lessons from Women of Stubborn Hearts

Copyright © 1975, 1977, 2015 by Stichting Manninne. All rights reserved.

A NavPress resource published in alliance with Tyndale House Publishers, Inc.

NAVPRESS and the NAVPRESS logo are registered trademarks of NavPress, The Navigators, Colorado Springs, CO. *TYNDALE* is a registered trademark of Tyndale House Publishers, Inc. Absence of ® in connection with marks of NavPress or other parties does not indicate an absence of registration of those marks.

The Team:
  Don Pape, Publisher
  Caitlyn Carlson, Acquisitions Editor

Cover design by Jacqueline L. Nuñez

Cover photograph of woman copyright © Linda O'Brien Photography/Getty Images. All rights reserved.

Cover illustration of wreath copyright © MarushaBelle/Shutterstock. All rights reserved.

All Scripture quotations, unless otherwise indicated, are taken from the Holy Bible, *New International Version,*® NIV.® Copyright © 1973, 1978, 1984, 2011 by Biblica, Inc.® Used by permission. All rights reserved worldwide. Scripture quotations marked ESV are taken from *The Holy Bible,* English Standard Version® (ESV®), copyright © 2001 by Crossway, a publishing ministry of Good News Publishers. Used by permission. All rights reserved. Scripture quotations marked TLB are taken from *The Living Bible,* copyright © 1971 by Tyndale House Foundation. Used by permission of Tyndale House Publishers, Inc., Carol Stream, Illinois 60188. All rights reserved.

Library of Congress Cataloging-in-Publication Data

Karssen, Gien.
  Her name is woman : wanderers : lessons from women of stubborn hearts / Gien Karssen.
    pages cm
  ISBN 978-1-63146-412-6
  1. Women in the Bible—Biography.   2. Bible. Old Testament—Biography.   I. Title.
  BS575.K36934 2015
  220.9'2082—dc23   2015012168

Printed in the United States of America

21	20	19	18	17	16	15
7	6	5	4	3	2	1

I dedicate this book to my many friends within The Navigators organization around the world. The plan to write the Her Name Is Woman series began to ripen through my global contact with young women. I saw in them the same fascination for the lives of women in the Bible that I have.

I further remember many, many others, men and women, who through their teachings, example, and friendship have made an indelible impression upon my life. I think of the first Navigator I met years ago—Dawson Trotman, the founder of the organization—and of the many young people who have found a personal faith in Jesus Christ through the ministry of The Navigators recently.

They all have three things in common: a great love for God, a deep reverence for His Word, and a passion to share their lives with others. Two words are applicable to almost all of them: realism and enthusiasm.

Through my fellowship with The Navigators, the intense desire to be a woman after the heart of God grew within me. For this reason the women in this book are not just people of a dim, distant past, but real people, living and sparkling. It is my desire that every person who reads this book will be challenged in the same way to live wholeheartedly for God. It is my desire that they be encouraged and built up. And, at the same time, I trust this book will prove to be an instrument in their hands whereby they can help others.

Contents

Foreword

When I began doing research for my Bad Girls of the Bible series, Gien Karssen's *Her Name Is Woman* quickly became a favorite resource. Her ability to delve into the hearts and minds of these biblical characters is remarkable, and her careful handling of Scripture reveals her deep respect for God and His Word.

Gien is also a gifted storyteller, allowing us to flee beside Hagar into the wilderness, to turn back with Lot's wife, to long for children along with Rachel, and to admire handsome Joseph, as Potiphar's wife did. We watch Delilah deceive Samson, and see Peninnah's jealousy in action. We listen to Job's wife rail against God, and our hearts sink in dismay when Orpah chooses the false gods of Moab, rather than the one true God of the Israelites.

The bitterness of Michal, the black heart of Jezebel, the cruelty of Herodias, the cunning of Sapphira—all are brought to vibrant life in these pages.

Gien doesn't shy away from describing the sins these

"wanderers" indulge in, yet she keeps our eyes fixed on the goodness and mercy of God. Descriptive details from other passages in Scripture and thoughtful questions throughout each chapter help us understand the lives of these women more fully.

In the end, it's Gien's ability to bridge the centuries and apply these ancient cautionary tales to our twenty-first century lives that make *Her Name Is Woman* a timeless treasure.

Liz Curtis Higgs, author of the Bad Girls of the Bible series

How to Use This Study

Do you long for a meaningful life? Do you want to become whole and fulfilled? These inborn, inner urges originate from the commission God gave woman at her creation. He expects woman, an equal partner with man, to be willing to step into her calling. The spiritual side of a woman is extremely important.

The women in this book are not fictional. They are real. They lived in history and, in their desires and problems, in their hopes and ambitions, are living among us today. Though the Bible doesn't share the full extent of their stories, I imaginatively explore what these women may have been doing and feeling in the time and place in which God placed them, in hopes that you will connect with their journeys even further.

As you learn about each of the women throughout the Her Name Is Woman series, the central question you must ask is, What place does God have in her life? The answer to this question decides the extent of every woman's happiness, usefulness, and motivation to keep moving forward. If God is absent, or if He is not given His rightful place, then life is without true purpose—without perspective.

As you read this book, join with these women of the Bible to consider your attitude toward God. And I hope that as you get acquainted with these women, you will make a fresh or renewed start in getting to know the Word of God.

I trust that meeting these women will turn out to be an unexpected gift for you and that you will resonate deeply with their experiences—and I pray that they will show you the way to a richer and happier life with God and other people.

AS YOU BEGIN

You may approach this book in one of two ways. First, just read it. The stories are intended to draw you deeply into the life of each woman in these pages. But be sure to include the Bible passages referenced at the beginning of each chapter in your reading. They are an important part of the book and are necessary for understanding the chapter. Second, you may wish to discuss the book in a small group. Considering the subjects and questions with some other people will add depth and greater insight to your study of these women.

Scripture references at the bottom of many pages will help you dig deeper into the Bible's wealth of truth and wisdom. You may answer the questions throughout each chapter personally or discuss them with your group. You may also conduct topical studies of these women or research accompanying themes. Whatever your direction might be, this study will become richer as you discuss these women with others, especially after your own individual preparation. Whether you do this study on your own or with others, be sure to use a journal so you may record your thoughts on the questions and any other things God impresses on your heart through the course of this study.

SUGGESTIONS FOR BIBLE STUDY GROUPS

1. Start with a small group—usually with a minimum of six and a maximum of ten people. This way your group will be large enough for an interesting discussion but small enough for each member to participate. As your number increases, start a second group.

2. Before you start the group, decide how often you want to meet. Many people may hesitate to give themselves to something new for an indefinite period of time. There are twelve chapters in each book of the Her Name Is Woman series, so they may easily be used as twelve-week studies. However, these books can just as easily work as six-week studies (two chapters per week). Some chapters are longer and will take more time to work through, while others are short enough to be combined into a two-part lesson. Please note that the number of questions varies depending on the length of the lesson. Discuss what process will work best for your group.

3. Remember that a Bible study group should discuss the Bible. While many of the questions within this book

are designed to help women examine their individual faith journeys, Scripture informs every piece of the study and should be referenced as an integral part of the discussion. Each participant should prepare her study at home beforehand so each member may share her personal findings.

4. Stress the necessity of applying the lessons learned, and help one another in doing this. There is a far greater need for spiritual growth than for an increase of knowledge. "How can what I learned influence my life?" is a question each participant should ask herself.

5. Determine, before you start, to attend every meeting. Miss only when you absolutely cannot attend. If you can't attend, do the study anyway and make up for it at the next meeting.

6. Consider yourself a member of the group. Feel free to make a contribution. Lack of experience should not keep you from taking part in the discussion. On the other hand, resist the temptation to dominate the group.

SUGGESTIONS FOR LEADERS OF BIBLE STUDY GROUPS

- Be sure that you have given sufficient time to your own Bible study and that you have completed it.
- Come prepared. Make notes of the points you want to stress.

- Begin and end on time. Set the tone by starting promptly at the first meeting.
- Few mountain climbers enjoy being carried to the top. Leave the joy of climbing to the group members. Don't do all the talking. Guide the discussion in such a way that each member of the group can participate.
- Don't allow any one person to dominate the conversation. Gently guide the group so each person may have an opportunity to speak. Sometimes it is necessary to talk privately with an overtalkative person, explaining the necessity of group participation. While some women may prefer to remain quiet, give them the opportunity to participate by asking them specific questions.
- Use the questions throughout each chapter as a jumping-off point, but feel the freedom to focus on issues that seem to particularly resonate with your group. However, don't allow the group to get too off topic. If a particular question becomes too time consuming or detracts from the overall study, redirect the conversation back to the main study. Getting back on track when the subject begins to wander can be done by saying, "Perhaps we could discuss this further after the study," or "Let's return to the main focus of the study."
- At the beginning of each session, open with prayer. Pray that Christ will speak to each person present by His Word. At the end of each session, pray for yourself and for each member of the group. Pray that the Holy Spirit will make you sensitive to the needs of others.

1

HAGAR

A Woman Who Rejected the God Who Saved Her

If she has given a maid to her husband and she has borne
children, [and] afterwards that maid has made herself
equal with her mistress, because she has borne children her
mistress shall not sell her for money, she shall put a mark
upon her and count her among the maidservant.

FROM THE LAWS OF KING HAMMURABI

READ

Genesis 16:1-16; Genesis 21:1-21

• • •

HAGAR PLODDED SLOWLY along the rough path. Her chafed
feet and ankles hurt with each step, and the seams of her
long robe were frayed and torn. Her heart beat quickly from
the exertion of the long journey; her eyes burned from the
scorching glare of the sun.

The wilderness in which she walked day after day offered
no protection. During the day terrible heat rose off the sand
in vapors, and the fierce wind blew dust into her mouth
and nose. At night the temperature dropped, and the land
became bitterly cold.

Despite the risks, Hagar pressed on toward Egypt, her home country. She wanted to return to the place where Sarah, the wife of Abraham (as they were later named), had bought her about twenty-five years before, then taking her to Canaan as a slave.

While she walked, she reflected on the years that had passed. They had been good years. Even though a slave girl, she had enjoyed a good life. *After all,* she thought, *I have been privileged to live with Abraham and Sarah, with whom God has even made a special covenant.* Through their example, she had come in contact with the living God.

Despite the good memories of her past, no thoughts of gratitude stirred Hagar's mind now. Far from that! Feeling that she had been wronged and even insulted, she was bitter.

In a strange way, Hagar was suffering the consequences of a bad situation in Abraham's household. When he had moved from the land between the Euphrates and the Tigris Rivers to Canaan, God had promised him a son. Through that son, Abraham was told that he would become the father of a multitude of nations.[1]

But years passed and the son didn't come. Worried, Sarah got the idea that the promised child should be born to a concubine, a second wife, instead of to her. According to the laws of that time, such a practice was allowed. In fact, a baby born of this arrangement was legally considered to be the child of the true wife and as such a rightful heir. In order to carry out such a plan, Sarah considered Hagar, who

---
[1] Genesis 12:1-5

occupied a favorable position within the family circle. After Hagar became Abraham's second wife, it was not long before she told him the happy news: "I am pregnant!"

Before Hagar's pregnancy, Abraham, since he had no son,[2] had thought that the male head of his household, Eliezer, would be his legal heir. But now, through Hagar, the child God had promised him might once again be coming into sight. Though Abraham had reason to expect that his heir would be a son of Sarah, up to that point God had never mentioned to him who the mother would be. He waited thirteen years for God to give him the answer.[3]

Before long, it was evident that Sarah's solution had been a purely human one. God's blessing toward Hagar had never been asked for and was not given. Impatient and doubting God's ability to work her situation out, Sarah had chosen her own way, and Abraham had given in to her plans too readily. No wonder the peace of God had left the house.

Reflect on a time when you made a decision out of impatience that impacted not only you but others in your life. What was the result?

At this time in history, a childless woman was despised by all. Unfortunately, Hagar didn't miss an opportunity to communicate such feelings toward Sarah. Then, as now, few

[2] Genesis 15:2-5
[3] Genesis 17:15-16

things in the world were so subtle and yet transmitted so clearly as the feelings of one woman toward another.

Is there a woman in your life whom you have negative feelings toward? In what ways do you treat her that might communicate a lack of love?

Sarah in turn reacted to Hagar's nonverbal communication. She, too, knew her weapons and how to use them. As the mistress, she had the oldest and first rights, a fact confirmed by the laws of her time. Even now Hagar remained Sarah's personal possession, to do with as she pleased.

What "weapons" do you use against people? Why?

Unable to approach Hagar without Sarah's permission, Abraham likewise could not prevent Sarah from using her power to humiliate Hagar.

Although all three of them had trespassed God's laws and were equally guilty in His sight, it is understandable that Hagar's attitude hurt Sarah deeply. This hurt partially explains Sarah's terrible treatment of Hagar. Yet knowledge of Sarah's inner turmoil does not make Hagar's humiliation any easier for us to accept.

Hagar, tiring of Sarah's treatment, finally lost her patience. Without asking permission, she fled to the wilderness. In this way she was true to her name. *Hagar* literally meant "flight."

Knowing full well that she and her yet-unborn child might be heading toward death, she disappeared into the wilderness. Alone and without food, she knew that she might never reach her homeland. Her child might never see life. But she had to try.

Often in the midst of difficult situations, we feel the urge to flee. Have you ever felt this way? What did you learn by staying?

Instinctively she began walking south on the long road toward Egypt. The farther she walked, the more her danger dawned on her. She had given up a sheltered community for the endless, inhospitable wilderness. Neither person nor beast could be seen for miles; there was no one to help her.

Somewhere in the northeastern section of the Sinai Peninsula, Hagar reached a desert spring along the road to Shur. The oasis offered refreshment and rest, but it did not still her inner needs.

Separated from security and friendship, she cried out from her innermost being to the God of Abraham, the only One who could save her. And He had not abandoned her. The slowly moving dot in the rough desert terrain of the

Sinai had not escaped His attention. He had kept His eye on Hagar just as He continues to do for all mankind.

"Hagar," He called loudly, addressing her by her first name.[4] He knew precisely who she was.

"Servant of Sarai," He added, placing her into the framework through which He saw her. In His eyes, she was still Sarah's maid. He did not begin the conversation with a rebuke, though under the circumstances He could have.

"Where have you come from, and where are you going?" He then asked. It was a disarming approach that gave Hagar room to speak her mind freely. Jesus Christ, who during His years on earth would use the same approach, was speaking to her.[5] Jesus Christ Himself was visiting her in the person of the Angel of the Lord. It was one of the preincarnate appearances of the Lord Jesus in the Old Testament.

"Where have you come from, and where are you going?" This question speaks to the larger picture of our lives. Consider your past and the path you are following toward your future. How does your relationship with God speak into both of those areas?

Later, He would reveal Himself in the same manner to Abraham, the father of all believers,[6] and to Moses,[7] both of

[4] Genesis 16:7-9, ESV
[5] John 4:4-42; 8:3-11
[6] Genesis 17:4-5
[7] Exodus 3:2-6

whom the Bible calls friends of God.[8] Both Jacob and Gideon would also be deeply impressed when they met Christ under similar circumstances.[9]

But Jesus Christ's first documented meeting with a person was with Hagar, long before He came to earth to redeem mankind. A young heathen woman who did not belong to the people of God, she—the mother of an unborn child—had come before God in extreme need. God in turn showed her the way to deliverance. In humility and repentance, she obeyed Him and turned back toward Abraham's camp. Her sin, like that of Eve, was pride. Renouncing her proud spirit of rebellion and willful independence, Hagar returned to Sarah, her mistress.

Instead of asserting herself or speaking out for her own rights, Hagar had to humble herself. The Lord Himself had given her an example of humility when He had stooped down to speak with her. Later, He would humble Himself much more in order to provide sinful people with an alternative to death.[10] He would give new life to everyone who personally trusted in Him.

In what circumstance or area of your life is God calling you to humble yourself?

God, who gives special blessings to those who have the courage to humble themselves,[11] honored Hagar's obedience.

[8] James 2:23; Exodus 33:11
[9] Genesis 28:12-17; Judges 6:11-23
[10] Philippians 2:5-11
[11] 1 Peter 5:6

"You will give birth to a son," He said. "You shall name him Ishmael ['God hears']. . . . I will increase your descendants so much that they will be too numerous to count."[12]

The son she expected would not be an easy man with whom to get along. He would have a wild and untamed character. Yet how she must have rejoiced in her heart at these words of God. There was hope again. Instead of expecting death, she now had the perspective of life. The future was blossoming for her and her unborn child. Jesus had a plan for their lives and had come down to share it with her personally.

"You are the God who sees me!" she exclaimed in adoration and worship.[13] Yet she was also afraid and overawed. *I have seen God and am still alive*, she thought after God left her. I *am able to tell others.*

The Bible tells of other appearances of the angel of the Lord (Genesis 32:24-30; Joshua 5:13-15; Judges 6:11-24). What were the reactions of these people, and in what ways are they similar to Hagar's?

Later, the spring oasis where she encountered God was named Beer Lahai Roi,[14] which translated means, "the well of the Living One who sees me." Hagar had experienced the true God who saw and answered her during her time of need.

[12] Genesis 16:11, 10
[13] Genesis 16:13
[14] Genesis 16:14

As long as Hagar lived, she no doubt remembered this experience with God. Every time she pronounced Ishmael's name, she reminded herself of this fact: The living God had heard and had acted.

Approximately seventeen years passed. Ishmael had now become a strong young man. Isaac, the son of promise, had now been born and at three years of age was finally ready to be weaned.

The weaning of a child during this time was cause for much celebration, for it was considered to be a milestone in the youngster's life. Abraham's entire household and many of his friends from neighboring cities came to celebrate and to see for themselves the miracle God had performed for Abraham and Sarah. One hundred-year-old Abraham and ninety-year-old Sarah had been blessed with a son in their old age, the son of promise from whose offspring the Messiah would later come.

But the party atmosphere was not entirely pleasant. Ishmael, the oldest son, could not tolerate all the attention his younger brother was receiving and began to mock him. There was, of course, more going on behind the scenes than just an innocent rivalry between two brothers. Ishmael, the son of natural birth who was procreated in unbelief and impatience, felt inferior to Isaac, the son of promise. Unwilling to accept second-place billing, Ishmael refused to acknowledge Isaac's privileged position. Unaware of God's promises to his mother in the wilderness many years before, Ishmael could not accept his subservient position.

Abraham loved both boys equally, as only a father could. Only Sarah understood what was at stake. "Get rid of that slave woman and her son," she demanded of Abraham. "That woman's son will never share in the inheritance with my son Isaac."[15]

In response to his wife's strong statement, Abraham became upset and confused. As he prayed, God showed him that the separation of his sons was necessary. The patriarchal line of the tribe God had chosen for His future people, Israel, would run through Isaac. He alone was the son of God's promise[16] and would become the forefather of a family of twelve tribes. From that point on, Abraham came to understand the difference between both sons had to be clear. Sarah was right. But through this confusion, God's promise to Hagar that her posterity would become great remained valid. Like Isaac, Ishmael would become the father of a family of twelve tribes because he was a son of Abraham.[17]

Thus Abraham had to send Hagar and her son away into the wilderness. After living in Abraham's household for nearly thirty years, she was now forced to leave. As Abraham filled up a water skin for Hagar, all three of them realized that the food and water for Hagar and Ishmael would not last long. Nevertheless, the difficult journey began.

The inevitable came all too quickly. The water supply ran out, and despite their frenzied searches, Hagar and Ishmael could not find a spring. Ishmael, weakened from walking and dehydration, was the first to fall to the ground, exhausted.

---

[15] Genesis 21:10
[16] Galatians 4:22-23
[17] Genesis 25:12-16

When it became clear that her son would soon die, Hagar used the last of her strength to drag him beneath a small but sheltering bush. It was the final service she could render to her child. Having done all she could do for her beloved son, Hagar could not bear to sit and watch him suffer any longer. Numb with fatigue and pain, she sat down some distance away and cried as if her heart would break.

Suddenly from heaven she heard the same familiar voice she had heard in the wilderness so many years before. Once again, the angel of the Lord asked her a question: "What is the matter, Hagar? Do not be afraid; God has heard the boy crying as he lies there. Lift the boy up and take him by the hand, for I will make him into a great nation."[18]

Startled, she looked up and saw a well of fresh water only a few feet away. Struggling to her feet, she hurried over and refilled the water skin. With the water God had provided, her son drank in new life.

For the second time, Jesus Christ had visited Hagar in her misery to save her life and the life of her son. Again, there had been the promise of a hopeful future for Ishmael.

As Ishmael grew older, his mother traveled to Egypt and brought him back a wife. By this act, she proved that she was still not a God-follower. Her extended time around Abraham and Sarah had not completely changed that. Even the visitation by Jesus Christ had not really changed her heart. The Lord on whom she had called in her need, who had helped

---
[18] Genesis 21:17-18

her, had not become the Lord of her life. He was not allowed to possess her heart.

Have you allowed the Lord to possess your heart, or do you simply call on Him when you're in need? What does it look like to allow God to be Lord of your life?

Because the Lord knew that Hagar would choose the idols of her past, He permitted her forced departure from Abraham's family. Instead of enjoying a sheltered and secure existence near Abraham, she chose to live a nomadic life in the desert. Because of Hagar and Ishmael's dreadful choice to assert themselves instead of living by faith in Abraham's God, the entire history of the world has been affected. Ishmael became the founder of the Arab nations, while the Israelites are the descendants of Isaac. The enmity of these two races still continues today.

Yet, despite everything, Hagar stands in history as a proof that Jesus Christ loves people. Every man, woman, and unborn child is loved by Him. His demonstration to Hagar proves that every person in need who calls out to Him will be answered. Jesus Christ, who was willing to reveal Himself to a woman who had reached the end of her possibilities, even now is available to everyone who seeks Him.

2
LOT'S WIFE

A Woman Who Did Not Take the Grace of God Seriously

The mountain ridge of Sodom consists entirely of rock salt. One of its forms remotely resembles a female figure. Tour guides still point to this as being the pillar of salt into which Lot's wife was changed.

THE AUTHOR

READ

Genesis 19:1-17; Genesis 19:24-26

• • •

NEARLY TWENTY CENTURIES AFTER CHRIST, Israeli buses arrive and depart from the southwestern shore of the Dead Sea. Tourists from all over the world come to see the original site of Sodom and Gomorrah, which the Arabs still call *Bahr Loet*—"the Sea of Lot."

Not much is to be seen. Sodom is more an experience than a tourist attraction. There is no trace of life. No color brightens the landscape. The surface of the lake, about a quarter mile below sea level, is the lowest spot on earth and evaporates quickly in the nearly unbearable high temperatures. The air vibrates from the heat and is heavily laden with odors of salt and sulfur.

In this oppressive and desolate atmosphere, it does not require much imagination to realize that a catastrophe once took place here. It is as if judgment still hovers over the land.

Centuries earlier, on the other hand, this same site was pleasant, green, and full of life.[1] Business in Sodom and Gomorrah had been conducted as usual, and there was little indication that the judgment of God was coming.

Despite its peaceful surroundings, on the evening of the day God had appointed, the bustling city of Sodom was in an uproar over two men who had come into town to visit Lot and his family.

Did Lot's wife know that her guests were angels sent by God to judge the city? She probably did not know how fervently the patriarch Abraham had pleaded with God to save the cities of Sodom and Gomorrah if they had but a few righteous inhabitants.[2] "The outcry against Sodom and Gomorrah is so great and their sin so grievous," God had said to Abraham, "that I will go down and see if what they have done is as bad as the outcry that has reached me. If not, I will know."[3]

But Lot's wife did know that life in Sodom had been immoral for years. The situation had become so bad that the male population of the town—young and old—had run out to rape her husband's guests.

---

[1] Genesis 13:10
[2] Genesis 18:23-33
[3] Genesis 18:20-21

She watched her husband leave the safety of their home to try to bargain with the unruly, violent crowd. She became upset when Lot offered her two virgin daughters to them in exchange for the two men, but from that point on the situation began moving too quickly for her to comprehend.

First the Sodomites turned their anger against Lot so furiously that only a miracle, an intervention by the men of God themselves, saved her husband's life.

Then she listened while the two men asked Lot several serious questions. "Do you have anyone else here?" they asked. "Sons-in-law, sons or daughters, or anyone else in the city who belongs to you? Get them out of here, because we are going to destroy this place. The outcry to the LORD against its people is so great that he has sent us to destroy it."[4]

At first she thought that the visitors were only trying to scare Lot unnecessarily. But they had saved her husband from the mob, and so she began to pay more attention to their words.

Her husband, too, listened and began to obey. He ran out the door and tried, unsuccessfully, to persuade his future sons-in-law to flee the city with him and his family. How he pleaded with them, only to become frustrated and humiliated when their laughter echoed in his ears. They thought he was joking and looked at him as though he had lost his senses.[5]

[4] Genesis 19:12-13
[5] Genesis 19:14

Scripture exhorts us to "listen to advice and accept discipline, and at the end you will be counted among the wise" (Proverbs 19:20). Is there an area of your life in which you are avoiding or discounting wise counsel?

Perhaps Lot's wife managed to get a few hours of sleep before dawn while her husband was still outside. But with the first faint glow of morning, the two visitors awakened her with urgent cries. "Quick, quick! Leave the city while you still can. Otherwise you will be destroyed with it," they told her husband.[6]

She looked hesitatingly around her—at her husband, at her daughters, at her home. *Why should I leave my home?* she asked herself. *Living in this city, in this house, is good, is it not? I am familiar with everything. My husband has an honorable position on the city council, and my daughters are engaged to be married. Life is taking its natural course as usual. Nothing has really changed. Why should God's judgment suddenly come on us now?*

Had Lot's wife moved out of Mesopotamia with Lot and his family years before? Or did Lot meet her much later in Sodom? Her background is unknown, just like her name. But whether she was born in Sodom or not, the city now controlled her thinking. Her heart was attached to Sodom.

---

[6] Genesis 19:15, author's paraphrase

The Bible does not say whether she had a personal relationship with God. Yet because of her marriage, she had become a close relative of Abraham, whom the Bible calls "the father of all who believe."[7] Abraham and Sarah lived in Hebron, which was quite near Sodom. No doubt she had met them, and through them had heard about God.

Lot, her husband, also knew the Lord God. But in the proportion that he grew attached to Sodom, he increasingly turned away from Him.

In what ways are you too attached to the sinful world around you? Spend time in prayer and allow God to convict your heart about how you can be in the world but not of it.

At this moment of her life, God made His decision. He could not allow the wickedness of Sodom to go on any longer. He had to punish the city because of its grave and shameless sins.

Despite His anger, God's heart was moved toward Lot's wife and her family. He wanted to save her from the claws of death that were already outstretched toward the city. He wanted to render grace to her, to offer her a favor that she didn't deserve. He even sent His angels to her doorstep to try to save the few people who did not need to be destroyed.

[7] Romans 4:11

But she wavered. She wasted precious time. The angels waited impatiently for her to move but finally could not linger a moment longer. The cup of God's wrath was filled to the brim, up till the last drop. Every second they waited meant playing with their lives.

God had done everything He could to save Lot and his family. Even though Lot's love for his Lord had cooled off, God still considered him a righteous man.[8] But now the family had to listen to His messengers and take their warnings to heart. They had to leave their city of sin behind.

What "city of sin" is God calling you to leave behind? Is there an area, attitude, or relationship in your life that draws you away from God?

Suddenly one of the angels grasped the hand of Lot's wife and led her out the door of her own home. His voice urged her on: "Flee for your lives! Don't look back, and don't stop anywhere in the plain! Flee to the mountains or you will be swept away!"[9]

Time having run out, Lot and his family left their home. When they reached the outskirts of the city, Lot asked permission to stay in the small, nearby city of Zoar. The angels granted his request, but urged him to avoid wasting any time. "Flee there quickly," one of the angels stated, "because I cannot do anything until you reach it."[10]

------

[8] 2 Peter 2:7-8
[9] Genesis 19:17
[10] Genesis 19:21-22

So the family left for Zoar. According to Eastern custom, Lot went first. His wife followed a few steps behind.

They had scarcely reached the little city when judgment broke loose. Sulfur and fire rained down from heaven on Sodom and Gomorrah. Nature's forces lashed the two cities violently, turning them into ashes. The entire region was wiped away from the face of the earth by the hand of God. No human being, no animal, no little blade of grass or small shrub remained alive.

When heaven's violence burst loose, Lot's wife gave proof that she had not taken the voice of God seriously. She looked back. Her feet had stepped away from Sodom, but her heart still lingered there.

In what ways are you "looking back" at past sinful patterns or environments? Lay your heart before the Lord and ask Him to help you keep your eyes on Him.

That look became fatal to her. The rain of sulfur and salt overtook her, covered her, suffocated her, and became her grave. Twelve words from the Bible describe her story. "But Lot's wife looked back, and she became a pillar of salt."[11]

She could have escaped death, for God had warned her in time. But she did not take His warning seriously. She ignored His grace, thus committing a grave error. To use

[11] Genesis 19:26

David's words, she cared nothing for God or what He had done.[12] The words of Isaiah might also be directly applied to her: "When grace is shown to the wicked, they do not learn righteousness; even in a land of uprightness they go on doing evil and do not regard the majesty of the Lord."[13]

Have you ever chosen to ignore grace?
What was the result?

That negligence cost Lot's wife her life. She didn't allow God to save her. She didn't accept the saving hand that He had stretched out toward her. She died because of her unwillingness to obey and act on faith, rather than because of the sins of Sodom. She had received the grace of God in vain.[14]

What does Scripture tell us about
grace? Consider Job 33:14,17-18 and
2 Corinthians 6:1 in your response.

Jesus later used her as an example of warning. "Remember what happened to Lot's wife!" He said to His disciples, in view of the final judgment still to come.[15]

Lot's wife has passed the point of being saved. Her doom

---

[12] Psalm 28:5
[13] Isaiah 26:10
[14] 2 Corinthians 6:1
[15] Luke 17:32, TLB

has been sealed. Yet her memory can still be a blessing if people who read her story are willing to accept the grace God is still offering. There is a fullness of grace in Jesus Christ,[16] and people who believe in Him receive grace, an undeserved gift of God.[17]

There is hope for every human being who takes what the Bible says seriously: "We must pay the most careful attention, therefore, to what we have heard, so that we do not drift away. For since the message spoken through angels was binding, and every violation and disobedience received its just punishment, how shall we escape if we ignore so great a salvation? This salvation, which was first announced by the Lord, was confirmed to us by those who heard him."[18]

---

[16] Ephesians 1:7-8
[17] Ephesians 2:8
[18] Hebrews 2:1-3

3
RACHEL

A Woman Who Was Attractive on the Outside
but Disappointing on the Inside

There are two kinds of beauty. There is a beauty which God gives at birth, and which withers as a flower. And there is a beauty which God grants when by His grace men are born again. That kind of beauty never vanishes but blooms eternally.

ABRAHAM KUYPER, *WOMEN OF THE OLD TESTAMENT*

READ

Genesis 29:1-30; also read Genesis 30–33; 35

• • •

SOMEWHAT CONFUSED, Rachel glanced at the foreigner who stood next to the well. She had met him only minutes before when she had driven her sheep there for a drink. As she neared the well, she watched in amazement as the stranger single-handedly rolled the heavy stone from its mouth with ease. The job usually required the strength of several strong men.

Even though she had never seen the man before, he did not appear a total stranger to her. Something about him was familiar. Moments later she understood why; he introduced himself as her cousin. He was Jacob, the son of Rebekah, her aunt, who had moved years ago from her home to Canaan in order to marry Isaac, his father.

He thinks that I'm beautiful, she thought as she stealthily observed the way in which he looked at her. This thought was nothing new to Rachel. She was used to attracting attention with her pretty face and lovely figure and had learned to accept the homage paid her beauty matter-of-factly. But the way this man was looking at her was different. His penetrating eyes contained a sparkle of awakening love, and his kiss of greeting had seemed to mean more than an impetuous gesture of a newly arrived relative.

Does your view of your outward appearance dictate your feelings about yourself and your response to others?

Captivated by Rachel's beauty from the first moment he saw her, Jacob did have a deep and growing love for his pretty cousin. He demonstrated his interest in her a month later by becoming a member of her father's household.

"You are a relative, all right, but that doesn't mean that you have to work for me without pay," Laban said to Jacob. "How much do you want to earn? Just name your price."[1]

No hesitation rang in Jacob's answer. "I'll work for you seven years in return for your younger daughter Rachel," he said resolutely.[2] He loved Rachel and was willing to do much in order to get her as his wife. Although seven years was a long time, for

[1] Genesis 29:15, author's paraphrase
[2] Genesis 29:18

Jacob the many weeks and months seemed to dwindle into just a few days because of his tremendous love for her.

And Rachel? What were her feelings during this time? Did she love Jacob in the way that he loved her? The Bible does not tell us about her feelings, nor about her reaction to the terrible event that occurred at her wedding, although it must have been utterly painful to her.

Laban, thinking about what suited him best, did not mind using crooked means to reach his goal. He deliberately took advantage of Jacob's passionate love for Rachel in order to marry off his unattractive older daughter, Leah, first. By exchanging his daughters, Laban tricked Jacob into marrying Leah instead of Rachel.

Jacob expressed his anger about Laban's deception in harsh words the following morning, but there is no record of Rachel's reaction. Hadn't she longed those seven years for him just like he had longed for her? Did the exchange of the brides bring sorrow to her heart? What were her inner thoughts? Was her outward beauty a resemblance of the beauty of her heart? Her reactions to the circumstances of her life provide the answers.

How do your reactions to the circumstances of life illustrate your inward spirit?

A week after the wedding, Jacob was married again, this time to Rachel, on the condition that he would serve Laban seven more years.

A marriage of one man with two women had special problems that were even more intensified since the women were sisters. Thus Rachel and Leah did not escape the tensions accompanying such an undesirable situation, and the fact that Jacob loved Rachel and not Leah made matters worse.

Leah, who experienced the pain of living with a husband who didn't love her, took her need to God. God, in turn, rewarded her with six sons and a daughter. Deprived of outward beauty, Leah's inward beauty grew under pressure, and she showed a reverence for God.

Rachel, on the other hand, reacted differently, pitifully. Her character left little room for gratitude and empathy. Jealous of Leah, she thought only of herself. To her, it was a matter of fact that she was privileged above Leah, that Jacob loved her, and that she was attractive. Yet concentrating her thoughts on the children she lacked, Rachel begrudged Leah her motherly happiness. In her heart, Rachel refused to accept the fact that she lagged behind her sister at this point.

In what things do you find your sense of purpose and identity? Often it is easy to place identity in relationships, talents, or other outward things, rather than in Christ. If you have struggled with this, how does finding purpose in things other than Christ impact your perspective?

"Give me children, or I'll die!" she exclaimed to Jacob bitterly.[3] These heartless words rudely revealed the place that Jacob held in her heart. She preferred death over her shame. Jacob apparently was not worth much to her.

Her exclamation also dishonored God. Although Jacob pointed out that Rachel addressed her complaint to the wrong person—God alone gives or keeps the blessing of children—he could not convince his wife.

The pain of unfulfilled desire did not drive Rachel to God. Instead, she initiated her own forced solution. "Take my servant-girl Bilhah as your wife," she advised Jacob. "Her children will then be counted as mine."[4] She was aware of the old custom that would allow Bilhah's children to be legally regarded as hers and thus Jacob's true offspring.

When Bilhah's son was born, the event gave even deeper insight into Rachel's character. "God has vindicated me," she said, and then named the baby Dan.[5]

Although she mentioned the name of God, it is evident that for Rachel the child was part of her competition with Leah. Rachel had claimed her rights; having lagged behind her sister in childbirth, she wanted to change her status.

This thought became even clearer when Bilhah's second son, Naphtali, was born. His name meant "wrestling," representing what Rachel felt was a growing victory in the fierce contest with her sister. Rachel was being motivated by bitterness, a dangerous and infectious attitude that has always affected people and their environments negatively.[6]

[3] Genesis 30:1
[4] Genesis 30:3, author's paraphrase
[5] Genesis 30:6
[6] Hebrews 12:15

Have you allowed bitterness to seep into any part of your life? If so, write a prayer asking God to uproot that bitterness. If not, write a prayer asking God to protect you from bitter thoughts.

When Rachel brought a concubine into the marriage, she started a dangerous chain reaction. Before long, Leah did the same with her servant girl Zilpah. At this point—as if problems were not big enough already—the family consisted of one man with four wives.

How deeply Rachel was touched in her soul by her husband's love remains unclear in Scripture. But it is evident that she manipulated his love in her competition with Leah. As the years passed, her jealousy remained. She did not give room to feelings of sympathy for her sister, who kept hoping to win Jacob's love. The words "give me" were uppermost in her thoughts.

One day during the wheat harvest, Rachel revealed her selfish attitude. Noticing that Reuben, Leah's first son, had brought his mother some fruit, Rachel wanted some too. Mandrakes were believed to aid fertility. They were scarce, and thus Reuben's find was rare. "Give me some of your son's mandrakes," she urged. "Then Jacob may sleep with you tonight."[7] Condescendingly, Rachel distributed love like merchandise in order to please herself. Keeping the reins of

---

[7] Genesis 30:14-15, author's paraphrase

the family and her husband in her hands, Rachel proudly manipulated them to gain her own ends.

Have you ever been guilty of manipulating relationships for your own ends? What was your motivation for doing that? What did God convict you about in that situation?

Apparently she did not know the real meaning of love. The vibrating warmth that could have been an outflow of love seemed foreign to her. What she knew best of all was self-love. The outward beauty that made her attractive made a painful contradiction when placed against her inner hardness and pride. Rachel's interest was frozen into a chilling circle around her own person.

When the real issues and values of life are compared, Rachel lagged behind Leah, whose life was controlled by God to a much greater degree. But that didn't prevent God from extending His goodness toward Rachel. Miserable, human egotism could not curtail the grace of God. The Lord saw Rachel's struggle. Knowing her passionate desire for a child of her own, He gave her a son, Joseph. When she named him, she proved once again how deep-seated her feelings of lagging behind her sister were.

"God has taken away my disgrace," she remarked. She then continued, "May the LORD add to me another son."[8]

---
[8] Genesis 30:23-24

Rachel remained the same old Rachel, even after her own son was born. Her thoughts remained egotistical, jealous, and ungrateful. "Give me, give me," was still her repeated life song. Her spirit of competition choked her gratitude, for those two attitudes could not live in her heart at the same time.

Consider a recent blessing from God in your life. How did you respond to that blessing?

Yet something in the patriarchal home changed after Joseph's birth. What the children of Jacob's other wives could not do, the son of his beloved Rachel did. Jacob became homesick for his father's land. After fourteen years of toil, he lost his willingness to work on foreign soil for someone else. Although his father-in-law convinced him to stay a little longer in Haran, Jacob started building the future of his own tribe. After six additional years of hard work—during which he became rich—he decided definitely to return to Canaan.

On that day, Jacob called Rachel and Leah to his side. He explained to them how the Lord God had commanded him to start the journey back to his homeland. Both wives agreed with his decision. "Do whatever God has told you," they answered unanimously.[9] Both women would gladly go with him. There was no conflict over his decision.

[9] Genesis 31:16

It is remarkable to see, however, how one single occurrence can reveal the inward being of a person so sharply. Special circumstances that interrupt someone's daily routine have the tendency to strip that person of all his or her false strengths and attitudes.

*What false strengths and attitudes
need to be stripped from your life?*

A change of this sort affected Rachel as she prepared for the long trek to Canaan. Naturally, such a trip was a big step for a young Eastern woman who had never left the boundaries of her village. The journey would be long, and the future country was unknown.

How has God used change to impact your growth?

The fact that God had given Jacob the call to depart and the encouraging assurance of His nearness proved to be no guarantee for Rachel. Many years of being married to Jacob apparently had not brought her nearer to his God.

Obviously her husband's love had given Rachel little inspiration to get to know him very well. His deepest thoughts remained foreign to her, and she didn't share his spiritual life. Although Jacob's character did have some striking flaws—his manipulation of business deals and his deceit—his faith in God always triumphed.

As Rachel's long-standing securities began to fail her, she clung to something she could hold on to—the household idols of her father. While Jacob was on his way to renew a covenant with God, Rachel was seeking refuge in pagan images.

In what idols of this world do you find comfort? How can you shift your thinking to turn more quickly to God in times of trial?

Leah, who also had been born and educated in this land where idols were served, had developed a growing confidence in God instead. She, unlike Rachel, had grown to trust the God of her husband, Jacob.

While the large family prepared to leave in secret, accompanied by the animal herds, Rachel stole her father's idols. This act shed even more light on her relationship with Jacob, for she committed the theft without telling him. She did not share her burdens with him. Despite Jacob's great love for Rachel, husband and wife never achieved real closeness and communication in their married life.

By stealing the idols, Rachel risked her life. Jacob was so insulted when Laban accused him of having stolen his household gods that he angrily replied, "If you find anyone who has your gods, that person shall not live."[10]

---
[10] Genesis 31:32

Rachel then used a lie to escape death. Seated on her camel saddle under which she had hidden the idols, she found a clever, acceptable excuse. Pretending indisposition because she was a woman, she did not leave her seat when Laban searched her tent. Thus Laban was unable to find the idols. Rachel's deception remained undetected, but her deed and the stolen images defiled the religion of the family of the patriarch Jacob. Later the harmful results of her act would be seen.

The Bible is not vague about God's view of the human heart. It clearly describes the heart in many different chapters. The human heart is bent toward evil "from childhood."[11] The heart is so deceitful, sick, and complicated that only God really knows it.[12] He calls it "stubborn and rebellious"[13] and says that those who are "proud of heart" are disgusting.[14] Truly God will not tolerate a sinful, unclean heart. David, Israel's greatest king, later expressed an understanding of these facts when he prayed, "Create in me a clean heart, O God."[15]

We are unable to change our own hearts. No matter how much effort we expend, we cannot reform our hearts ourselves. Only God can do that. Therefore He invites all of us to give Him our hearts,[16] to allow Him to work.

Yet God often allows people to suffer in order to change their stubborn, self-willed hearts and bend them toward Him—not in spite of His love, but because of it. He tests men and women to see if they are prepared to do His will.[17]

[11] Genesis 8:21
[12] Jeremiah 17:9-10
[13] Jeremiah 5:23
[14] Proverbs 16:5
[15] Psalm 51:10, ESV
[16] Proverbs 23:26
[17] Deuteronomy 8:2, 16

Using a study Bible or online study resource, research what Scripture says about the heart. What does the Bible teach you about our hearts in relationship to God?

In light of these facts, Rachel's heart was not exceptionally bad or unusually self-willed. Instead of surrendering her life to God, she chose to govern her own life. That wrong decision of self-rule led to egotism and multiplied her personal problems.

Since God's love did not have the chance to light her heart through, it remained blocked up in darkness and the cold of pride could hardly release warmth. When we want to share our hearts with others, we first have to surrender our hearts to God. Only then do we receive and share God's love.

Rachel's desire to prove herself in motherhood led to her death. Before Jacob and his family definitely settled in the Promised Land, Rachel died in childbirth. With her last breath, Rachel named her baby son Ben-oni, which meant "son of my sorrow." But Jacob later renamed the baby Benjamin, "son of my right hand."[18]

Despite Rachel's seriousness and unhappiness, a ray of hope still existed in her older son, Joseph. He was still young when his mother died, but he grew up to be an exceptional man of God in whose life God had absolute preeminence.

---
[18] Genesis 35:18

He was destined to become an extraordinary blessing to the Hebrew people.

Shortly before Rachel died, Jacob renewed his covenant with God. He removed all foreign idols from his household and buried them. After this purification had taken place, God so closely aligned Himself with Jacob and his family that all his neighbors were deeply impressed. Despite all the past mistakes, a new beginning with God had taken place.

Did Rachel's heart go out to God in the last phase of her life? Did the motherless boy, Joseph, become the product of his father's education? Or had Rachel changed enough through God's power that she was able to make an indelible impression upon him?

Whatever the answers, Rachel's pitiful and unfulfilled life could have been exciting and full of meaning if only her inner beauty had matched her lovely outward appearance.

4

POTIPHAR'S WIFE

A Woman Swayed by Sex

According to biblical thinking, two human beings who have
shared the sexual act are never the same afterward. They
can no longer act toward each other as if they had not had
this experience. It makes out of those involved in it a couple
bound to each other. It creates a one-flesh bond with all
its implications.

WALTER TROBISCH, *I MARRIED YOU*

READ

Genesis 39:1-20; 1 Thessalonians 4:3-5

• • •

POTIPHAR'S WIFE HAD EVERYTHING. She had a husband who
held a high-ranking position as an officer to Pharaoh.[1] She
lived in a spacious and luxuriously furnished home. She
wallowed in wealth, with food and clothing in abundance.
She oversaw an extensive household staff, who provided her
slightest wish. She was a spoiled woman.

As an Egyptian she also enjoyed greater liberty than many
other women of her time. One could conclude that she would
be very happy. But the situation was really quite different.

[1] Genesis 37:36

It has been said that situations don't make us—they reveal us. This is true of Potiphar's wife.

———

What does your attitude in your current situation reveal about you?

———

She appears in Scripture in connection with Joseph, the male head of her husband's household. Joseph, the son of Jacob and Rachel, was a strikingly handsome man who had arrived in the house of Potiphar after being sold into slavery by his brothers.

But Joseph's inner life was more remarkable than his good looks, for he had a close walk with God. Several times God had revealed Joseph's future to him in dreams. That was one reason his brothers had been jealous of him. They had felt he looked upon them with disdain. When they had further realized that their father favored Joseph, their fury reached its limit. They got rid of him by selling him to passing merchants.

It soon became very clear that God was with Joseph, however, for wherever Joseph went, the blessing of God followed. Thus, Potiphar's house was blessed—because of Joseph. A relationship of mutual appreciation and respect grew up between Joseph and his master. Consequently, Joseph's responsibilities increased until, finally, he was in charge of the entire household.

Potiphar's wife, who at first glance seemed to possess everything a woman could desire, was inwardly empty, a woman without purpose. She had too much time on her hands. She was married to a man to whom work meant everything. While the Bible doesn't mention any children, if there had been any, a nurse would have most certainly cared for them.

Perhaps her feelings were hurt because her husband did not give her the attention she desired. An empty life searches for fulfillment, and an empty heart craves satisfaction. Potiphar's wife ultimately gave expression to desires that were in her heart.

Have you ever experienced an empty life?
Where did you seek fulfillment during that time?

Didn't she realize that it was Joseph's inner character of beauty, righteousness, and fidelity that was attractive, not just his physical appearance? Couldn't she understand that the special thing about him was his close walk with God?

Evidently not, for she humiliated herself and Joseph—not once, but repeatedly. She imposed herself and her body upon him. She expected to find satisfaction in sex alone. She didn't know that the sensation she craved would only produce passion, an emotional excitement that would consume her if the act was not grounded in love and the security of marriage.

In creation God said, "That is why a man leaves his father and mother and is united to his wife, and they become one flesh."[2] So God has included sexuality forever in the warmth, security, and love of marriage. This is clear by His order— the becoming of one flesh was to be a result of love. The decision to leave one's parents—starting a household—provides the proper environment for the culmination of sexual love. Without these prerequisites, sex is a lust that consumes and can degrade a human being to a low animal level. This results in self-accusation, loneliness, and shame. It creates a still greater loneliness, for the craving for more sensual passion has been established. Finally utter desolation results. It becomes a vicious cycle of misery.

What is your view of sex? How does that impact your relationships?

The trouble ahead for Potiphar's wife could not be overlooked, and she certainly could not find a solution to her problems in sex. Sexuality, used in this manner, creates its own hell.

Joseph immediately put the temptation into proper perspective.

He did not minimize it, but called it what it was: sin. He spoke of the great respect he felt toward her husband. But his greatest concern was God. "How then could I do such a wicked thing and sin against God?"[3] he asked. Joseph was right; every act of sexual intercourse outside marriage is a sin

---

[2] Genesis 2:24
[3] Genesis 39:8

that God abhors. Immorality is one of the deadly weapons that comes straight from hell and destroys the person who indulges in it. Joseph knew this well because he walked with God. He knew what displeased the Creator.

"But a man who commits adultery has no sense; whoever does so destroys himself. Blows and disgrace are his lot, and his shame will never be wiped away."[4] While Solomon wrote these words many years later, Joseph understood and applied this principle in the situation with Potiphar's wife.

The fact that Potiphar's wife didn't know the God of Israel was no excuse. She was trespassing a law of life that God gave to humankind in creation.[5] She proved this when she twisted the truth after Joseph had rejected her. She accused *him* of the immorality she had intended to commit herself! Joseph's hasty flight, which gives proof to his purity of character, exposed her even more and twisted her mind. Being his superior, she decided, without any scruples, to ruin his career and stain his good name.

Read 2 Timothy 2:22 and 1 Corinthians 6:18.
What do these verses teach us
about fleeing from sin?

This ushered in a difficult time for Joseph—a stay of many years in prison. He undoubtedly felt very hurt by the dishonest

[4] Proverbs 6:32-33
[5] Romans 2:14-15

accusations. He probably felt forsaken, too, since Potiphar apparently did not investigate the situation. Evidently, however, Potiphar didn't believe his wife, or he would have certainly had Joseph put to death.

Joseph didn't complain. To his joy he found that even prison walls could not keep God away. God was still with him, as He had been in Potiphar's house. Again Joseph was a blessing to those around him. He was finally rewarded for his loyalty to God and his master and given rule over all of Egypt. He was second in command to Pharaoh, the ruler of Egypt. He became Zaphenath-paneah, the protector of the people. Eventually he was able to save the brothers who betrayed him when they were threatened by starvation.

Joseph was not the loser.

Potiphar's wife was.

Nothing more is heard about her—not because of the magnitude of her sin, but because she showed no sorrow and asked no forgiveness. She appeared to desire no knowledge of God, even though He was so willing to give her joy and satisfaction in life that He had touched her life through the person of Joseph.

She could have found victory over her sexual desires if she had recognized them as sin in time. She could even have regained control of her mind and body after Joseph's first rejection of her. She could have asked Joseph about the God who was governing his life.

Idleness became the soil that nourished her sinful thoughts. Only after she succumbed to her evil thoughts was she then confronted by the desire to sin in deed. Since deeds are the fruit of thoughts, her thoughts were the source of her downfall. A person becomes what he or she thinks. The temptation of Potiphar's wife was not unusual. Millions of people today are being tempted in the same manner, because Satan continually goes about like a roaring lion, seeking "someone to devour."[6] He will never change his character.

---

*Study James 1:13-15. What desires are
in danger of leading you into sin?*

Potiphar's wife allowed her temptation to grow into sin because she did not curb her desires, but rather allowed them to entice and draw her into an actual sin.[7] She had no desire to correct herself.

She had the time, the intelligence, and the potential to use her life positively, but failed. Therefore, no good word can be said about her. It is tragic that she lived without having left behind any positive impression.

[6] 1 Peter 5:8
[7] James 1:14-15

5

DELILAH

A Woman Who Deliberately Ruined a Spiritual Leader

I find more bitter than death the woman who is a snare, whose
heart is a trap and whose hands are chains. The man who
pleases God will escape her, but the sinner she will ensnare.

ECCLESIASTES 7:26

READ

Judges 16:4-30

• • •

DELILAH WAS A PHILISTINE WOMAN who belonged to a cul-
ture that worshiped idols. She was also a woman who didn't
take morality seriously. Having little respect for her body, she
threw away her honor casually, like a prostitute.

The Bible doesn't mention these facts as clearly as it does
about Rahab,[1] but the context does allow these conclusions.

Delilah is remembered as a woman who ruined a spiritual
leader. What motivated her to damage Samson so irreparably?

Samson was an extraordinary man, a servant of God. He

---
[1] Joshua 2:1

45

was called a Nazirite, a man dedicated to God even before his birth.[2] His long hair demonstrated this commitment, and for twenty years he ruled and judged over his Israelite people.[3]

Samson's name, which meant "little sun," showed how happy his parents had been when he was born. His birth, like that of Jesus many centuries later,[4] was announced by an angel. It was also the result of a miracle, since his mother initially could not have children. After his birth, Samson developed under the blessing of God into a leader—the mightiest man of Judah—and possessed unusual physical strength.[5] Thus he was far ahead of his enemies, who rightly considered him to be unconquerable. Hadn't God said that Samson would begin to deliver Israel from the hand of the Philistines?

Despite his physical strength, Samson was morally weak. The man who easily ripped a lion apart with his bare hands had no control over his sexual passions. Samson had loosened the necessary brake on his behavior toward the opposite sex, a move that is dangerous for a man and destructive for a spiritual leader.

*Read James 3:1. Why are leaders
held to such a high standard?*

Different women before Delilah had already exerted a bad influence on his life. Now he fell into her hands and became

[2] Judges 13:2-5, 24-25
[3] Judges 15:20
[4] Luke 1:26-38
[5] Judges 14:5-6; 15:13-16

involved. He didn't marry her. He didn't take her as his wife into his own house. Instead he became her lover and lived with her.

The leaders of the Philistines, probably one for each of their large cities, heard about Samson's relationship with Delilah. So they drew Delilah into a conspiracy to cause his downfall. After all, it had become a national necessity for them to kill Samson. Where military force had failed, slyness now had to succeed.

The leaders visited Delilah personally and said, "See if you can lure him into showing you the secret of his great strength and how we can overpower him so we may tie him up and subdue him."[6]

Was it Delilah's love of money that made her accept the proposal? Each of the men promised her 1,100 pieces of silver. Since every piece weighed over sixteen grams, the total weight of silver promised would be an inconceivable sum.

The love of money is a real danger. Moses stated that a person who accepts a bribe becomes blinded,[7] and Paul called the love of money "a root of all kinds of evil."[8] Those who seek money for its own sake become pierced with many sorrows.

How do you view money? Are there any ways in which you may have let the love of money creep into your life?

---

[6] Judges 16:5
[7] Exodus 23.8
[8] 1 Timothy 6:10

Or were Delilah's actions caused by bitterness against the Israelites? Samson's future as a leader of a nation that had always proven itself stronger than her people because of God's help now lay in her hands. The God of Israel was not her God, for she and her people worshiped the idol Dagon.

The request of the Philistine leaders also must have appealed to her pride. In a country and period of history where a woman's position lagged far behind a man's, the important leaders of her country were knocking on her door for help.

Do a quick study on what Scripture says about pride. What are the dangers of pride, according to God's Word?

After she accepted their proposal, Delilah went about finding the secret of Samson's strength. She began her deceit with every means that she as a woman had at her disposal. Her first step was flattery. "Please tell me what makes you so strong," she begged. "Is there anyone who could ever capture you?"[9]

Blinded by his feelings for Delilah, Samson unwisely answered her. He clearly underestimated the danger he was in. If he had been in close contact with God, he would have become alarmed and quickly left her.

Through Delilah's insolence, the leaders of her people witnessed her humiliating game with Samson from an adjoining

[9] Judges 16:6, author's paraphrase

room. They listened intently as she bound him with seven raw-leather bowstrings. Then she called out, "'Samson, the Philistines are upon you!' But he snapped the bowstrings as easily as a piece of string snaps when it comes close to a flame."[10] The leaders, realizing that the plan had failed, remained where they were.

Delilah then worked on Samson's honesty. "You are making fun of me," she said, sulking. "You told me a lie."[11] Samson once again listened to her and played her dangerous game. But once again the ropes with which she had tied him broke like spiderwebs when he used his muscles.

Living with a man who proved that he cared about her did not change Delilah's thoughts. It did not soften her character. On the contrary, everything she had—her allurement, her brains—was willfully and unchangingly directed toward Samson's destruction.

Again she continued her attempts to trap Samson, this time by weaving his hair into her loom. Once again she had no results. Although the Philistine leaders had become impatient and returned to their cities, Delilah had enough patience left to try one more plan of attack.

Now she played the role of a woman whose feelings of love had been hurt. "You say that you love me," she whined, "but you don't confide in me. You have betrayed me these three times now, and you still haven't told me what makes you so strong."[12]

---

[10] Judges 16:9
[11] Judges 16:10, author's paraphrase
[12] Judges 16:15, author's paraphrase

She based her new attack on her passionate lover's reaction when his love was doubted. Daily she sulked, nagging at him without interruption. Constantly she accused him about his tricks.

_____

How does your treatment of others change when you feel rejected? What should be your response? Consider Romans 12:20 and Matthew 5:44.

_____

She knew how to use this final weapon with conviction and with success. Gradually she broke Samson's resistance. He became like wax in her arms. Finally, utterly frustrated, he could not stand it any longer. He could think of only one thing: *I want to stop this sulking. I want peace!*[13]

Then he told her the whole truth. "My power is connected with my long hair. It has never been cut," he confessed. "Since before my birth I have been dedicated to God. My strength lies in my commitment to Him. My hair is a symbol of that. Cut off my hair and I am no different from any other man."[14]

Sensing that this time Samson was speaking the truth and was not holding anything back, she relentlessly sent a message to the Philistine leaders. "Come back once more," she said. "He has told me everything."[15] At no time did she have second thoughts about betraying her lover.

[13] Judges 16:16
[14] Judges 16:17, author's paraphrase
[15] Judges 16:18

Have you ever betrayed someone? If so, what was your motivation? Have you ever been betrayed by someone you trusted? What did God sharpen in your character through that experience?

The men came quickly with their money. Once again they hid themselves. Again Delilah did what Samson had told her to do. She called in someone to cut off his seven locks of hair while he was sleeping on her lap. Even while the hair was being cut, Delilah felt that she had won. When his hair dropped to the ground, Samson's strength left him.

When Delilah screamed out, "Samson, the Philistines are upon you!"[16] for a moment Samson didn't realize his defeat. Like the other times, he tried to shake himself free. But this time his struggles were in vain. After his hair was cut, the Lord left him.[17] He lost his tremendous strength—and the presence of God—through his own mistakes.

The results were appalling. The Philistines captured Samson. They didn't kill him, but they gouged out his eyes. From then on he went through life mutilated; empty sockets saw nothing but darkness.

As a token of their triumph and Samson's shame, the leaders sent him to the city of Gaza. As if the humiliation of his blindness and imprisonment were not enough, he was put to work grinding grain like a common slave. Samson, a servant

[16] Judges 16:20
[17] Judges 16:20

of God and a ruler in Israel, was tarnished. A deeper degradation for this giant could hardly be imagined.

His people shared his suffering. After Samson's rule ended, they entered a period of defeat, anarchy, and spiritual decline. His tarnish became theirs.

Samson had denied his God, his ideals, and his people. He had become a betrayer of himself and the cause for which he stood. Naturally he only had himself to blame for his deeds. But that did not make Delilah any less guilty. Like Samson, Delilah was personally responsible before God for her deeds. She remained accountable for her share in the disaster that struck Samson and others.

Is there any unconfessed sin in your life for which you are accountable? Lay it before God.

The only fact that could be mentioned in Delilah's defense is that she didn't know God. She didn't have His laws. Yet, even as a heathen woman, she had little excuse.

Solomon, nearly two centuries later, characterized the relationship between Delilah and Samson: "I find more bitter than death the woman who is a snare, whose heart is a trap and whose hands are chains. The man who pleases God will escape her, but the sinner she will ensnare."[18]

Delilah's actions also align with the portrait of the bad woman Solomon warns about in Proverbs: "For the lips of

---

[18] Ecclesiastes 7:26

the adulterous woman drip honey," he writes, "and her speech is smoother than oil; but in the end she is bitter as gall. . . . Her feet go down to death."[19] And Delilah's feet did indeed lead to death.

The city leaders were overjoyed. To celebrate their capture of Samson, they declared a great festival dedicated to their god Dagon. Once the festival had begun, the people became excited and called for Samson. They wanted to make fun of and humiliate him. They wanted to exalt Dagon over the God of Israel. When Samson finally arrived, didn't anyone notice that his hair had been growing? Was there no one who had carefully watched this man who had once been undefeatable?

The large festival building was completely filled with men and women and, of course, the Philistine leaders. Probably even Delilah was there, for how could they celebrate such an enormous feast without the heroine? Just the flat roof of the building held about three thousand people.

Was there no one in the crowd who remembered the God of Israel and of Samson? Was there no fear that He would avenge the insult paid to Him, His servant, and His people?

When the Philistines forced Samson to stand between the two pillars supporting the roof so that they could mock him, Samson remembered his former calling. Wasn't he appointed to redeem his people from their enemies? "Sovereign LORD," he prayed, "remember me. Please, God, strengthen me just once more, and let me with one blow get revenge on the Philistines

---
[19] Proverbs 5:3-5

for my two eyes."[20] At the same time he pushed against the pillars with all his might, and they crumbled. The entire building crashed down, killing Samson and thousands of Philistines.

The catastrophe Delilah had brought about and through which she probably lost her life undoubtedly reached much further than she had anticipated or desired. What had begun with immorality ended with the deaths of many people. The outcome of her deeds was worse than the beginning.

"An adulterous woman is a deep pit,"[21] Solomon wrote. "None who go to her return or attain the paths of life."[22] Close fellowship with someone deep in sin is like scooping fire into one's lap.[23] Can anyone do that without being burned?

In her book *The Unique World of Women*, author Eugenia Price writes that the Christian women of today possibly feel themselves far removed from the treacherous and vile Delilah. They are, she believes, convinced that they have nothing in common with Delilah. Eugenia then warns women not to make a serious mistake: "We may not be harlots, or even overtly conniving and deceitful as Delilah was, but many of us *are* deceitful. . . . In fact, I think all of us have streaks of deception."[24]

What "streaks of deception" have you allowed
to creep into your life? Search Scripture
for words to combat those deceptions.

---

[20] Judges 16:28
[21] Proverbs 23:27
[22] Proverbs 2:19
[23] Proverbs 6:27
[24] Eugenia Price, *The Unique World of Women* (New York: Bantam Doubleday Dell, 1969), 83.

Centuries after Samson's and Delilah's deaths, Paul gave another warning to the Christians in Corinth that also applies to our perspective concerning Delilah's life: "Now these things occurred as examples to keep us from setting our hearts on evil things as they did."[25] It is wise not to ignore these warnings.

---

[25] 1 Corinthians 10:6

6
PENINNAH

A Woman Conquered by Jealousy

Leading health authorities have determined that the deeper cause of much illness is in the emotional reactions to life. Prolonged bitter hatred can damage the brain, and can cause heart disorders, high blood pressure and acute indigestion—all severe enough to kill a person.

ROBERT D. FOSTER, *STUDIES IN CHRISTIAN LIVING*

READ

1 Samuel 1:1-8; Proverbs 6:24; Proverbs 14:30; Proverbs 27:4

• • •

PENINNAH LIVED IN A TIME OF DECLINE. Israel had arrived at one of the darkest points in her history. After Moses and Joshua had ruled the nation so capably, the time of the judges arrived.

God Himself wanted to rule. However, the people were little interested in God and increasingly turned toward serving idols. Thus theocratic rule failed.

The decline resulted in anarchy. The laws of the government were no longer obeyed. Every man was doing what was right in his own eyes.[1] The spiritual climate was no better than the political and social. The wrath of God was accumulating upon the head of Eli, the head priest, because he tolerated the bad behavior of his sons, Hophni and Phinehas.

Eli saw that they were eating the best of the sacrifices offered to God by the people. He knew that they degraded the tabernacle by engaging in sexual misbehavior, and though he rebuked their actions, his sons had not listened to him.[2]

It has been said that we judge those outside the church too much and those within it not enough. Do you feel comfortable calling other Christians to account? What does a righteous approach look like? (Read Matthew 18:15-20 and Titus 3:9-11.)

The judgment of God was at hand. The house of Eli had lost its influence, and the nation was about to be besieged by its enemy, the Philistines.

But even more dreadful than this was that God hardly spoke during these days. There was little communication between Him and His people.[3]

Peninnah lived during this period. Elkanah, her husband, had two wives. God meant for each man to have only one wife and each woman to have only one husband.[4] But, since

---

[1] Judges 21:25
[2] 1 Samuel 2:12-33
[3] 1 Samuel 3:1
[4] Genesis 2:18; Matthew 19:4-6; 1 Corinthians 7:2

people fell away from His ideal, He provided for these exceptions, mainly to protect the firstborn son.[5]

As Elkanah experienced, anyone who deviates from God's plans brings difficulty upon himself and others. The atmosphere in his home was unbearable. The fact that Peninnah had children while his other wife, Hannah, did not, just added fuel to the conflict. At least the form of religion had its proper place in Elkanah's family. But although every member paid his religious tributes, God was not real to Peninnah. She was discontented. She was not grateful to Him for her children and the other good things she possessed. Her life was paralyzed by a lack of thankfulness. It must not have dawned on her that God desired other tributes; for example, loving others. She had everything a Jewish woman could desire, because she had many children. This was generally a proof of God's favor. She would continue to live in the future through the lives of her children long after she was dead.

What specific things are you thankful for today?

On the other hand, Elkanah's other wife was heavily burdened by her childlessness. Hannah was not affected by the spirit of the times in which she lived. Because God was central in her thoughts, her deeds were inspired by faith. She was attractive and mild-mannered. Elkanah saw the difference

---
[5] Deuteronomy 21:15-17

between the two women clearly. He could not help but prefer Hannah over Peninnah.

But Peninnah was not inspired by Hannah's example. In fact, her response was just the opposite. She exalted herself over Hannah because she had given birth to children—many children. The fact that God was the One who had made it possible for her to have them didn't enter her mind.

What blessings has God given you? How can you give Him glory for those?

Peninnah was jealous of Hannah. She provoked her incessantly, especially when the Jewish holidays arrived. These days caused Hannah extra pain anyway because they were celebratory times for families, during which families from all across the nation came to the house of God in Shiloh. It seemed Peninnah was even more bitter toward Hannah during these days.

Have you ever experienced jealousy? What actions resulted from that attitude?

Peninnah had allowed her bitterness to take root in her heart.[6] And since she hadn't guarded her heart,[7] her life had become poisoned with envy. This envy stemmed from rivalry,

---
[6] Hebrews 12:15
[7] Proverbs 4:23

selfishness, and a lack of humility. Envy looks only after its own interests, not those of others. The Bible warns strongly against self-first attitude.[8] Envy is not one of those small character weaknesses that God will allow people to live with. He puts it in a list of sins that society considers to be far greater: adultery, idolatry, witchcraft, etc.[9]

How are envy and the other sins mentioned in Galatians 5:19-21 described? What strikes you as you compare the vice of jealousy with the others listed there?

"Jealousy makes a man furious,"[10] wrote Solomon. It is like a fire. If not quenched rapidly, it cannot be stopped because it affects other parts of the body. This is especially true of the tongue.[11] Peninnah is an example of how a person can use her tongue to vent her jealousy. Though it is one of the smallest members of the body, the tongue can cause a blazing flame that can destroy entire lives. No wonder that in such a case the Bible says a person misusing the tongue is "set on fire by hell."[12]

Jealousy devours a person because it stems from Satan. In fact, it destroyed Satan himself. He envied God. In his pride he wanted to be like Him, and this caused his downfall.[13]

---

[8] Philippians 2:3-4
[9] Galatians 5:19-21
[10] Proverbs 6:34, ESV
[11] Romans 3:14
[12] James 3:6
[13] Isaiah 14:13-15

Therefore, Satan is happy every time a human falls into this snare he has prepared. Often he has great success, for people are jealous by nature. It is ironic that people can allow the tongue, which they use to talk to God and to honor Him, to be inspired by Satan.

In what ways can you be more intentional about using your tongue to honor God?

Jealousy begins in the mind. If it is not arrested in time and brought to God,[14] it ruins one's thought life and hinders interpersonal relationships. It is also subtle. It is a far greater danger to the person who harbors it than it is to the person toward whom it is directed. Like a boomerang, it returns to the envious person. Peninnah experienced this. She did not manage to solve her problems, even while the solution was within her grasp. All she needed to do was observe and follow the example of Hannah's faith.

---

[14] 2 Corinthians 10:5

7
JOB'S WIFE

The Woman Who Said No to God

The main guilt of a man are not his sins. Temptation is powerful
and his strength is weak. The main guilt of a man is that he can
turn any moment to God and neglects to do that.

RABBI BOENAM AND MARTIN BUBER,
FOUNTAINS OF JEWISH WISDOM

READ

Job 1:1-3,6-12; Job 2:1-10; Job 42:10-13; Romans 8:28

• • •

THE WIFE OF JOB LIVED IN THE LAND OF Uz, in Arabia, probably not far from Ur of the Chaldeans, the city where God
called Abraham. Few women were as privileged as she was.
Her husband was immensely rich. Their royal household contained many servants. She had seven sons and three daughters.
They were all wealthy and had pleasant, frequent meetings
with one another. They even conducted regular family parties
to strengthen their mutual bond. But the greatest of her blessings was her husband, Job.

Job was a man who loved God. All he knew about God was what others had told him, but that was sufficient to cause Job to serve Him devotedly. The depth of Job's spiritual life accounted for the warm atmosphere in their home. His life was so permeated by this God-centered devotion that people around him were aware of it. People said that Job was a devout man and that this was the reason he was prosperous. The foundation of Job's wife's life was the piety and prosperity of her husband and household.

_____

*What do you know about God that causes
you to want to serve Him devotedly?*

_____

This was the situation on earth.

Something remarkable took place in heaven at this time. Job was the subject of a conversation between God and Satan. God was pleased that Job, a man on earth, loved Him voluntarily. God was looking for people like Job, who was fulfilling the purpose for which God had created him—fellowship with Himself.

_____

*Read John 14:23 and 2 Corinthians 6:16. What
do you learn about God's relational heart?
How should that impact your view of Him?*

_____

Satan, the accuser of believers,[1] didn't agree with God's evaluation of Job. He contradicted what people on earth were saying about him. He felt that the reason Job was devout was that he was prosperous and suggested that if prosperity was withheld from Job, he would turn from God.

"All right," replied God. "We'll test your accusation, Satan. Take his possessions from him, but do not harm him."[2]

If you lost your most precious possessions or relationships, how would you respond?

Satan was devilishly happy with this arrangement and poured calamities upon Job. One terrible blow after another befell him. His enormous stock of cattle was either stolen or struck by lightning. Thus Job lost all his wealth. But the greatest catastrophe of all Satan reserved until last—he destroyed all of Job's children.

Everything Job had built over many years was gone in one blow. The richest man in the entire East was suddenly bereft and without children. All that was left to him, besides his home, were four servants—and his wife.

Satan had done his work thoroughly, but he still hadn't achieved his purpose. Although Job, in the custom of the East, did rend his garments, his faith in God remained unshaken. "I was born with nothing, and when I die I will

[1] Revelation 12:9-10
[2] Job 1:12, author's paraphrase

have nothing; the Lord gave, and the Lord has taken away; blessed be the name of the Lord," said Job.[3]

Satan and God talked once again about Job. God pointed out Job's continued loyalty. Satan reacted by saying that Job hadn't been harmed personally. Only his possessions and externals had been affected. "Let me inflict harm in his body," Satan said, "and then see if his faith will still stand."[4]

What would be the worse trial for you—external (possessions/relationships) harm, or internal (physical) harm? Why do you think that is?

God then allowed Satan to do what he wished with the single restriction that he could not take Job's life. Satan sent a disease so terrible it could drive a man out of his mind. Job was covered from the soles of his feet to the top of his head with itching, sore boils.

Medical science agrees that the suffering of such a patient would be unbearable—beyond one's imagination. The hideous disease drove him to the dung pit, where dogs rummaged for cadavers of animals and where the lowest of humans searched for what others had thrown away. There he sat and scraped his sores with a piece of broken pottery.

But then came the greatest blow of all. His wife turned against him. The woman God had intended to walk through

---
[3] Job 1:21, author's paraphrase
[4] Job 2:4-5, author's paraphrase

life with Job, the woman he needed now more than ever before, no longer supported him. Through her, Satan played his last card. "Do you still hold fast your integrity?" she asked bitterly. "Curse God and die."[5]

What sort of perspective do you communicate when someone else is suffering? When you are suffering?

She was so overcome by sorrow that she was only able to see one way out—to renounce faith in God and commit suicide. Her reaction was just the opposite of her husband's.

Job's faith endured even this crisis. The true situation may have been hidden from him, but he did not doubt God. God was still a reality to him. Therefore, he was able to accept both the good and the bad from Him. His life was built on a rock, and although storms beat against it incessantly, it wouldn't collapse. It was a foundation that would last.

As the roots of a tree are tested for strength in a storm, so the storms of sorrow and unexplainable experiences uncover the life foundation of a man. Job had a strong foundation; his wife did not. Naturally, her sorrows were extreme. It is hard to identify with her loss. She could have sustained herself if she had built her life on the same solid foundation as her husband. But their different responses to the situation were not due to the way they each experienced the sorrow, but to

---

their foundation.[6] Thus, she was unable to support her husband during the most difficult period of his life.

At least Job's friends came to visit him, though they were of no help. But the Bible doesn't record any attempts on the part of his wife to soften his pain. During the entire period of suffering she was never in the foreground of the story.

God has entrusted women with a unique talent to sympathize and to encourage others. But Job's wife didn't provide that support when he needed it most.

Suddenly and radically the situation changed again. Job and his wife again had ten children—seven sons and three daughters as before. His livestock was restored; in fact, he had even more cattle than before the catastrophe.

But Job's suffering had borne fruit far more important than these temporal things. His relationship with God had been deepened. "I had heard about You before," Job told God, "but now I have seen You."[7]

No longer did Job need to rely upon the experience of others, for he had met God personally. This led him to repentance and humility.[8] These two characteristics are inevitable results from a meeting with God.

Is your relationship with God based on what others have told you about Him, or on what you have learned from Him personally?

---

[6] Matthew 7:24-27
[7] Job 42:5, author's paraphrase
[8] Job 42:6

Job had received insight into himself and God. He understood that there needed to be a Mediator between God and man.[9] Thus the suffering had served a positive function for him. It had revealed to Job things he had never known before. Like Jacob, he had wrestled with God and prevailed.[10] The result was a richer and happier life.

And Satan? He was the loser again. The result of his tempting Job was exactly the opposite of what he had planned—Job was more dedicated to God than ever.

The Bible does not say much about Job's wife. It states that in the heat of temptation she had pointed to the wrong party—God—as being guilty. Like many unbelievers, she had been blinded by Satan.[11] She failed to understand that although God allows suffering, His aim is not merely that man should suffer, but that suffering should bear positive fruit.[12] Her finite foundation of security had been shaken in order for her to find the unchangeable happiness—God Himself. The road to finding this happiness, however, ran through the school of suffering.

As an Old Testament woman she naturally carried a doubly heavy load. She missed the encouragement of the written Word of God and she had no circle of Christian friends to support her. Yet she had living proof that it was not necessary to be defeated in a crisis, not even in her day. Her husband, Job, was that proof. The New Testament praises him because

---

[9] Job 9:32-35; 16:19
[10] Genesis 32:28
[11] 2 Corinthians 4:4
[12] Hebrews 12:11

he continued to trust in God in times of sorrow.[13] When Satan aimed his fiery arrows of temptation, Job used his faith like a shield, stopping them.[14]

What encouragement does the Bible offer to Christians who persevere in difficulties? Compare James 5:11, Hebrews 12:11, and 1 Corinthians 10:13.

He proved that no man is tempted so strongly that he cannot stand up against it and that God does show a way to escape in the midst of every temptation.[15]

Job had built his life upon God's foundation. But it appears that his wife could find no solid ground for her feet. Sorrow threw Job into the arms of God. But in the critical hour of her life, Job's wife said no to God.

---

[13] James 5:11
[14] Ephesians 6:16
[15] 1 Corinthians 10:13

8

ORPAH

A Woman Who Sank into Oblivion because of a Wrong Decision

Our lives will go on for millions and millions of years. And the choice we make now decides the type of life we are going to live in the future.

BILLY GRAHAM, *THE CHALLENGE*

READ

Ruth 1:1-15; also read the entire book of Ruth

• • •

LIFE HAD DEALT HARSHLY WITH ORPAH. As a young woman, she had already experienced a larger portion of suffering than many people do in a lifetime.

The death of her husband, Kilion, was the hardest blow to strike her. She had been a good wife for him, but their happiness had only lasted a few years. Since their marriage had been childless, after his death she was alone.

Within the circle of relatives, Orpah wasn't the only person who had experienced suffering. Naomi, her mother-in-law, was also a widow. Ruth, her sister-in-law, had shared the same experience. These three deaths had snatched away all the male members of the family. As a result, a close tie had developed among these three bereaved women.

———————

Consider those closest to you. What shared experiences have served to draw you together? What has God taught you through those relationships?

———————

Orpah and Ruth were continually impressed with the love and unselfish attitude of their mother-in-law. Naomi, who among them had lost the most, gave herself fully to their well-being instead of looking to her own interests.

But from now on Orpah would miss Naomi's loving care and the friendship and understanding of Ruth. The blessings that accompanied and softened her sorrow were now to be only memories, for Orpah had chosen to go back to her own people and to their gods.

We meet Orpah on a deserted country road somewhere in Moab, not far from the border of Israel. She was a lonely figure. When she looked back, she saw Naomi and Ruth moving away from her in the opposite direction. Then the horizon swallowed up the diminishing dots they represented. They were gone, forever separated from Orpah.

Only a short time before, the three widows had walked together in the direction of the Israelite border. Now Orpah shuffled back down the road toward her homeland, alone.

Naomi's decision to return to Bethlehem hadn't come as a surprise for Orpah. *Was my mother-in-law ever really happy in Moab?* Orpah wondered. *Even though she adjusted well to a foreign country, Naomi always seemed to be uprooted and dispersed.*

Orpah knew this because of Naomi's relationship with God. Naomi was a Hebrew and did not worship the idols that the nations surrounding Israel did. She worshiped the true God who had chosen the Israelites to be His own people[1] and who had specifically given them the land in which they lived.[2] It was clear to Orpah that Naomi would only be happy in her own country, the land where her God was worshiped.

Both Ruth and Orpah had shared Naomi's decision to leave Moab and had left with her without hesitation. The three of them, originally united in their love for Mahlon and Kilion, belonged together.

So they began their journey. While their feet moved forward on the hot and dusty road, each of them entertained lingering thoughts of the past. Orpah's thoughts were with Kilion, the man she had loved. She missed him, especially now that her future was so uncertain.

Then, suddenly, Naomi stopped on the road. "Why don't you go back to the home of your parents?" she asked. "That is better, Orpah and Ruth, than coming with me. May God bless you for all the love you have shown my sons. May He reward you with another happy marriage."[3] To show her daughters-in-law that they had to take her words seriously,

[1] Deuteronomy 7:6
[2] Deuteronomy 1:8
[3] Ruth 1:8-9, author's paraphrase

Naomi then kissed them good-bye. At that point all three of them burst into tears.

Ruth and Orpah didn't want to listen to Naomi's proposal. But Naomi's arguments were strong and logical. "Why should you come along with me? Your future lies within marriage. If you go with me, you will miss that opportunity. I am too old to have children," Naomi pleaded. "And, even if that were possible, because of their ages my sons would not be suitors for you."[4]

As they listened to this clear argument, both Orpah and Ruth began to cry again. But decisions became finalized. Ruth firmly decided to remain with Naomi, while Orpah, scared of the unknown future, was willing to be persuaded. After kissing her mother-in-law for the last time, Orpah turned around and began her journey back home. This is the last time that the Bible mentions her name.[5]

Read back through Ruth 1. What similarities of circumstances and attitudes do you see between Orpah and Ruth? What is the remarkable difference between the two?

The Bible does not mention Orpah's reasons for her decision. It is clear, though, that till her separation she had not distinguished herself from Ruth in any way. Both of them

[4] Ruth 1:11-13, author's paraphrase
[5] Ruth 1:14

are praised for their love toward their husbands. Both proved willing to leave their parental homes and their homeland to face an unknown future. Yet the circumstances changed when a personal decision was suddenly demanded of them.

How do you respond to the unknown? What fears do you have about an unknown situation in your life right now? What do you sense God teaching you about trust in Him?

Why did Naomi talk so urgently? Why did she paint the bare facts for Orpah and Ruth so clearly? Perhaps she knew that they would only be able to live happily in Israel if they had the chance to choose their new country voluntarily.

Through her own experiences, Naomi had learned that there was more than just a place to live or a person at stake. Their choices were choices for or against God, and as such had to remain individual decisions based on personal conviction.

Joshua, a leader of the Hebrew nation, had emphasized that point before. "Choose for yourselves this day whom you will serve," he had declared, "whether the gods your ancestors served beyond the Euphrates or . . ." He then added, "But as for me and my household, we will serve the Lord."[6]

Like Ruth, Orpah had come in contact with the God

---

[6] Joshua 24:15

of Israel through the Hebrews. Unlike Ruth, however, she decided not to serve God and was content to allow Him only to remain the religion of her husband and her in-laws. She did not want to accept Naomi's God as her God.

At the moment of decision, Orpah decided in favor of the god of her country, Chemosh, who was called "the detestable god of the Ammonites."[7] She preferred this god above the God of Israel. She chose a god who could not speak or act instead of the Creator of heaven and earth.[8] She turned her back on God—who wanted to show her His goodness—to serve vain idols.[9] She exchanged the God who gives life for an idol who claimed lives through child-sacrifices.

While we may be followers of God, we sometimes make choices that follow the "gods of our country"—letting other things dictate our perspective rather than God. What are some ways you may be doing this, or may have done this in the past?

"Orpah has returned to her people and her gods."[10] With these words of Naomi, Orpah sank into oblivion. Her name disappeared from biblical writings.

The Bible clearly teaches that our decisions have eternal

[7] 1 Kings 11:7
[8] Isaiah 16:12
[9] Jonah 2:8
[10] Ruth 1:15, author's paraphrase

consequences. And our decision whether to follow God determines our eternal destiny—whether we will spend eternity apart from God or with Him.

Perhaps Orpah later repented of her wrong decision and turned from her idols to God. If she sought to find Him with her whole heart, then doubtless He found her.[11] If, however, she did not seek God, then her future was over and she lost her life and her soul for eternity.

———

Study Orpah's life in light of Malachi 3:16-18 and Revelation 20:12-15 and write down your conclusions. What applications do you see for your own life?

———

———
[11] Jeremiah 29:13

9

MICHAL

A Woman Whose Marriage Lacked Unity and Fell Apart

The safe way for any marriage—as for any human relationship—
is the shared experience of God. We can disagree on any
number of other things and keep on loving, if we agree
about God.

EUGENIA PRICE, *THE UNIQUE WORLD OF WOMEN*

READ

1 Samuel 19:10-17; 2 Samuel 6:16-23

• • •

THE MARRIAGE OF MICHAL, the youngest daughter of King
Saul, did not enjoy a happy start. The marriage problems
had not developed due to the difference in social standing
between the king's daughter and the shepherd boy. Rather,
Saul had arranged David's marriage to Michal, hoping that it
would make David unhappy and cause his death.[1] Saul had
given his daughter to David in marriage because he wanted
him to die.

Saul could no longer stand the man who would become

---

[1] 1 Samuel 18:17-21

king in his place, the man who had already won the love of his people. On many occasions he had already tried to kill David, without success.

David, in fact, had earned the right to marry Saul's eldest daughter, Merab. The king had promised her to the man who would defeat the Philistine Goliath.[2] But David felt unworthy of marrying the king's oldest daughter, so the king gave her to someone else.[3]

Then Saul offered his youngest daughter, Michal, to David on the condition that David would kill a hundred Philistines. *The possibility that David could hold out against that many Philistines is so small,* the king thought grimly, *that he will surely lose his life.*

But Saul had excluded God from his thinking. Through God's blessing, the young man killed two hundred Philistines, and Michal became his wife.[4]

It is no wonder that Michal loved David. He was handsome, courageous, and sensitive. He was both a brave warrior and an artistic man who wrote songs and composed music. He was popular with the people and had been appointed to be their next king. The most striking characteristic of David's life, however, was his relationship with God.

Soon it became clear that David's being Saul's son-in-law had not changed the king's feelings. Again Saul began brooding about how he could take David's life. When he discovered that he could not get rid of David through war

---

[2] 1 Samuel 17:25
[3] 1 Samuel 18:19
[4] 1 Samuel 18:27

or his own weapon, he devised a plan to kill David in his own house.

Michal, however, heard about the plot. "If you don't get away quickly," she warned David, "you are a dead man."[5]

Thus she helped her husband escape in time. When the servants of her father came the next day to fetch him, he was gone. "He is ill," Michal lied,[6] probably to win time. That was the last drop in Saul's cup of fury. "Bring him up to me in his bed," he commanded angrily.[7] Soon he discovered that his daughter had deceived him. A disguised house god had been placed in the bed to look like David. It is uncertain whether David knew that this idol was in his home. But it was the first indication of a growing breach between Michal and her godly husband.

Consider your closest relationships.
In what areas are you lacking unity?
Why do you think this is the case?

Outwardly, their marriage seemed to have spiritual unity. Michal worshiped the God of Israel just like her husband. But in her heart, that God was a stranger to her; her relationship was not one of trusting Him. Her husband, on the other hand, did not worship other gods; his love for God was undivided and applied to daily situations.

[5] 1 Samuel 19:11, author's paraphrase
[6] 1 Samuel 19:14
[7] 1 Samuel 19:15

———————————

In your relationship with God, is your heart
undivided or divided? If your heart is undivided,
what kinds of things have the potential to
divide your heart? If your heart is divided, how
does that impact your daily life and actions?

———————————

Lack of spiritual unity in a marriage initially might seem to be only a scratch on marital happiness. But such a scratch often becomes a crack, which then widens into a gulf that cannot be bridged. The mutual life-house cannot be built on an uneven foundation. Such a marriage from the beginning lacks the solid base it needs to be happy and durable enough to survive the storms that are bound to come. No right-thinking person would risk moving into a house that either has no foundation at all, or that is built on a weak one. So it is unthinkable that the highly important choice of finding a life partner so often is done without consideration of spiritual principles that can stand firm against life's strains.

———————————

How much importance do you place on
sharing life with someone with whom you
share spiritual unity? Do you intentionally
invest in a vibrant relationship with God
so you may be such a partner?

———————————

When her father furiously accused her, "Why have you deceived me and let my enemy escape?" Michal replied, "He threatened to kill me if I didn't help him."[8]

These were revealing words. Instead of speaking the truth, Michal accused David in a terrible way. The man who before long would refuse to avenge himself by killing his father-in-law, the man whose conscience would disturb him when he only cut off the edge of Saul's robe, and who would restrain his men from killing his pursuer,[9] was here charged with an attempt to murder his wife.

Read Proverbs 6:16-19 and Luke 6:45.
What did Michal's words reveal about her heart?

Michal's acts differed greatly from David's. In the same situation, David threw himself upon his God, something he always did in trying circumstances. God was his refuge, and David expected the solutions to his problems to come from Him. Indeed, David's line of thought was completely different from his wife's unbelief and deceitful spirit.

The spiritual rift between David and Michal was becoming obvious. But what had happened also put a question mark on Michal's professed love.

David and Michal clearly traveled different roads. Predictably, after David's disappearance, their marriage terminated

[8] 1 Samuel 19:17, author's paraphrase
[9] 1 Samuel 24:1-7

abruptly. The cause was not, however, due to the absence of spiritual unity. In his desire to get revenge on David, Saul gave his daughter to another man in marriage—to Paltiel, the son of Laish, of Gallim.[10]

Years passed, and after David became king over Judah he called for Michal to return to him. What moved him to call for her?[11] The Bible is not explicit. Also, no mention is made of the feelings of Michal, who like a handball had been thrown from one man to another. No doubt her emotions were torn as she left her second husband and watched him weep in anguish as she slowly returned to David.

After this incident, we meet Michal one more time. Again years have passed, for David is now king over all of Israel. He had experienced the glorious high point of his life. God had fulfilled His promises. David's enemies were defeated, and his kingship was highly respected among the surrounding nations.[12]

Yet the crown on David's work was still to come. He had one more service to do for God. It was impossible for David to be happy until the ark—the proof of God's presence—arrived at its rightful place in Jerusalem, the capital.

When that day finally came, the whole of Jerusalem streamed together to receive the ark of the Lord in a festive manner and to bring it to the place David had appointed for it. The priests and the Levites had prepared themselves spiritually for their tasks. The singers and the musicians had already tuned their instruments. The leaders of the people

---

[10] 1 Samuel 25:44
[11] 2 Samuel 3:14-15
[12] 1 Chronicles 14:2

had taken their places in the procession and were joined by many from the population of Israel.

Suddenly an indescribable shout of rejoicing broke loose. Cymbals, trumpets, harps, and lyres competed with the voices of the people in praising God.[13]

The happiest person of all was King David. A deep gratitude swelled in his heart because God was allowing him this honor. David experienced the occasion not as the proud king but as a sinful person who was aware of the presence of a holy God.

In this situation, it was fitting that he put aside his royal robe and gird himself with the linen breeches that God had ordered priests to wear.[14] The great king rightly felt that he could only appear before God in the dress of a servant of the ark. He didn't merely want to be the peoples' authority, a man who blessed them with fatherly presents. He sought to identify himself with them. Before God, he was their equal, equally judged by Him. Their God was his God.

David then expressed his overwhelming joy and thankfulness in a religious dance. This dance, modeled after Eastern custom, visually demonstrated his feelings toward God.

What expression does your overflow of praise take? What are some other ways you can express praise to God?

---

[13] 1 Chronicles 15:3-25
[14] Exodus 28:42-43; 1 Samuel 2:18

Michal was missing from the crowd that moved out to receive the ark festively. Once again it became evident how great the breach between her and David really was. Michal didn't share the religious convictions of her husband. This great day, a highlight in his life, didn't impress her in the least. Like her father, Michal was not concerned about the ark of God.[15] She felt no desire to fetch a tambourine and lead the women in a song to the Lord as Miriam once had.[16]

Quite the contrary. Michal despised David because of his excitement and actions. From behind a window, she watched him at a distance as he danced among the common people. In her heart, she looked down on him.

_____

Have you ever looked down on someone?
What was at the heart of that attitude?

_____

When David returned home after the arrival of the ark, desirous to share the joy of the day's festivities with Michal, she approached him with a scornful, biting remark. "How glorious the king of Israel looked today!" she sneered. "He exposed himself to the girls along the street like a common pervert!"[17]

These words did not express thoughts about God. Michal despised the king, her husband, who could forget himself in such a way to identify himself humbly with his people. She

[15] 1 Chronicles 13:3
[16] Exodus 15:20-21
[17] 2 Samuel 6:20, author's paraphrase

had only biting sarcasm for a man who, in her opinion, had thrown his dignity away.

What is one difficult situation you're currently facing in which you feel tempted to dwell in a negative attitude? How can you instead express thoughts about God?

Michal was proud and cold of heart—toward God, toward her people, toward her husband. In her sarcasm she called David perverse and impudent. Not only did she reject his religion, she besmirched it. She called it immorality. Once again, Michal placed David in an unfavorable light.

The absence of love painfully revealed itself. Michal not only did not love her husband and her husband's God, but also lacked the love of one person for another. After many years of marriage, she still did not know her husband's heart. She did not consider the things that moved him. His motives were not hers.

The widening gap between husband and wife was not due primarily to differences of character or ambition. Rather, each thought and responded out of different religious frameworks. Her husband's obvious fear of the Lord had not kindled a desire in Michal's heart to experience the Lord God in the same way. Their many years of marriage had not touched her inner person spiritually.

How does this story illuminate
2 Corinthians 6:14-15?

Michal did not become a wife after David's heart because she was not a woman after God's heart. David felt closer to the simple women among the people—who loved God—than he did to his own wife.

The Bible does not record how long Michal lived after this incident, but it does imply that her married life was over. The rift between the partners was now complete.

"Michal [the] daughter of Saul had no children to the day of her death," says the Bible.[18] The conclusion could be drawn that after this incident David no longer went to Michal as her husband. Her role as his wife was over, and she spent the remainder of her days in loneliness. She died without having an influence and may never have met the God of her husband through personal commitment.

The marriage of David and Michal stands as a warning in history. If a husband and wife are not one in God—sharing spiritual unity—their marriage union may fold under life's pressures.

---

[18] 2 Samuel 6:23

10

JEZEBEL

A Woman Who Forgot That No One Can Trifle with God

Don't be misled; remember that you can't ignore God and get away with it: a man will always reap just the kind of crop he sows! If he sows to please his own wrong desires, he will be planting seeds of evil and he will surely reap a harvest of spiritual decay and death.

GALATIANS 6:7-8, TLB

READ

1 Kings 18; 1 Kings 19:1-3; 1 Kings 21:5-16

• • •

QUEEN JEZEBEL COULD HARDLY CONTAIN HER ANGER. As she rested in her summer palace in Jezreel, she listened intently to the report of her husband, who had just returned from a trip to Mount Carmel.

"You should have seen what Elijah did," King Ahab said, shaking his head. His wife had been expecting a different beginning to the tale of what happened when Elijah challenged the priests of the god Baal to measure their strength against the strength of his God. This story should not be about Elijah!

Jezebel was the daughter of Ethbaal, king of the Sidonians,[1] whose people lived in the country north of Israel. Her father was not merely king over his people—he was also a priest of Baal.

After Jezebel married King Ahab, she introduced the worship of Baal into Israel. This religion—crude and inhuman—was known for its child sacrifices. Because of Jezebel's influence, her husband surpassed everyone else in doing what was wrong in the sight of God. She "encouraged him to do every sort of evil."[2] She was firmly dedicated to the worship of idols.

Ahab, a weak man, became a willing instrument in Jezebel's hands and offended the Lord God more than any king before him.[3] The worst of his many sins was his marriage to the idol-loving Jezebel.[4] He, an Israelite king, began serving Baal—because of her and with her.

How do you respond when others try to exert influence over your faith or speak strongly about different beliefs?

Through Ahab's influence, Baal then took over the place of the living God in the Israelites' hearts. But Jezebel was not satisfied; she undermined the Hebrew religion till nearly all the people accepted Baal as their god. The queen began to

[1] 1 Kings 16:31
[2] 1 Kings 21:25, TLB
[3] 1 Kings 16:33
[4] 1 Kings 16:30-32

exercise more and more power over her husband, till finally she ruled the people.

Perhaps Jezebel herself gave the order to kill all the prophets of the God of Israel. But Obadiah, the foreman of Ahab's household, saved the lives of a hundred prophets by hiding them in a cave at the risk of his own life.[5]

Jezebel, however, continued to encourage the worship of Baal. She supported the prophets of Baal personally, feeding four hundred of them every day at her own table.[6]

In Jezebel's thinking, the God of Israel was equal to Baal. She considered Yahweh to be a local god who carried a message just for the Israelites. She was pleased that Israel's God had seemingly been unable to keep pace with her god, Baal, within His supposedly chosen nation. So when Elijah put forth the challenge to the priests of Baal, she was sure Baal would be victorious. Were her priests not in the majority? So 450 priests of Baal were matched against one lone prophet of the true God of Israel.[7]

Do you ever feel as though God is silent while the "gods" of this world are winning the day? What does this story teach you?

According to plan, two altars were built. One was for the Lord God, the other for Baal. The true God had to prove

---
[5] 1 Kings 18:4
[6] 1 Kings 18:19
[7] 1 Kings 18:22

Himself by sending fire to light the wood. No human being was allowed to kindle the fire.[8]

The priests of Baal began their ceremonies first, shouting until their throats were hoarse. When they hadn't received a reply by noon—no fire had come down on their altar—they wounded themselves terribly with knives and swords until blood gushed out. Although they continued to rave all afternoon, their god remained silent. He was a lifeless god, incapable of giving an answer even when 450 of his servants called on him in ecstasy.[9]

Then Elijah started repairing the altar of his God, the living God, which had been torn down. He worked alone, calmly stacking twelve stones, each of which represented one of the twelve tribes of Israel.[10]

To mark the contrast and at the same time to testify to his faith openly, he dug a trench around the altar about three feet wide. Then he arranged the wood and laid a bull on top. Four barrels of water were then poured over the sacrificial carcass and the wood. That ritual was repeated three times, clearly putting Elijah's God at a disadvantage.

After he finished all the preparations, Elijah walked up to the altar and pleaded, "Answer me, LORD, answer me, so these people will know that you, LORD, are God, and that you are turning their hearts back again."[11]

That very moment fire flashed down from heaven and

[8] 1 Kings 18:23
[9] 1 Kings 18:29
[10] 1 Kings 18:31
[11] 1 Kings 18:37

completely burned up the sacrifice, wood, water, stones, and even the dust. It was a breathtaking and awesome event.

There was no doubt who the true God was. The Israelite people who had glided away to idolatry came to their senses. Those who had shown no preference at the beginning of the contest were now convinced.

How do our lives manifest our belief in a powerful God? What might change in how you approach a difficult situation if you dwelt on God's power before responding?

"The LORD—he is God! The LORD—he is God!" they shouted.[12] Then fury broke loose against the prophets of Baal. Every one of them was killed next to a nearby brook; not one escaped.

Then the Lord God answered another prayer of His prophet Elijah. A drought that had harassed the country and its inhabitants for three and a half years came to an end after an announcement by the prophet. Rain that hadn't fallen during those years came down in showers from heaven.

"The water came so suddenly," Ahab said to Jezebel now, still obviously frightened, "that even though Elijah told me to leave immediately, I hardly reached the palace before the downpour."[13] As her husband told the story, Queen Jezebel became filled with rage.

[12] 1 Kings 18:39
[13] 1 Kings 18:41, 45, author's paraphrase

After Ahab finished his story, Jezebel was not impressed by the way in which the Lord had dealt with the priests of Baal. She considered His action to be a personal insult.

Naturally her fury unloaded itself on Elijah. In her mind, he was the only person who could be blamed for the recent event. Her words to him were bitter and full of hatred. "You killed my prophets. I swear that I am going to kill you," she stated. "Tomorrow you will be dead."[14]

So mighty was this woman—so evil, so ruthless—that Elijah did not doubt that she would execute her threat. The man who had calmly faced King Ahab and 450 excited prophets of Baal now lost all courage. He fled for his life into the wilderness. "I have had enough, LORD," he lamented, crouching under a tree. "Take my life."[15]

What do Elijah's action and request of the Lord in the wilderness suggest? When you feel hopeless, what do you say to God?

Happily the situation was not nearly as somber as the despondent prophet perceived it to be. There were still seven thousand people who had not bent their knees before Baal and broken their covenants with God.[16] But Elijah only heard about them later.

Jezebel probably thought that she had won a new victory over the living God. Either she did not get the chance to kill

---

[14] 1 Kings 19:2, author's paraphrase
[15] 1 Kings 19:4
[16] 1 Kings 19:18

Elijah or else she did not use her opportunity because she feared the people's reactions. But her enemy had taken flight, and she considered that a victory.

Now no one remained to take the side of God openly. Jezebel had come one step further in her goal to extinguish the worship of Israel's God. Her growing perception of victory made her presumptuous—almost reckless—as she soon demonstrated.

During this time, Ahab began to desire a vineyard that bordered his palace and was owned by a man named Naboth. Wanting to use the piece of land as a royal garden, he offered to give Naboth a good price or a better vineyard for it. Naboth refused. The land was his father's inheritance, and Israelite law forbade him to part with it. The property had to remain in the family. Naboth knew that if he parted with it he would be disobedient to the Lord.[17]

Ahab understood Naboth's response, for he knew the Lord's commandments. Yet he sulked about the refusal like a child who didn't get what he wanted and refused to eat. He went to bed, sullenly, and turned his face to the wall.[18]

———

Reflect on a time recently when you did not get your way. How did you respond? Did your response emerge from selfishness, or from trust in God? Why?

———

[17] 1 Kings 21:1-3
[18] 1 Kings 21:4

Jezebel thought her husband's response was utterly stupid. In her homeland no authority ranked higher than the king. "A nice king you are," she railed. "Do you rule this country or not? Get up and eat. Be happy. I'll get you Naboth's vineyard."[19]

Jezebel was an unscrupulous woman who could commit murder without the slightest remorse. Thus she started looking for an acceptable excuse to kill Naboth. After his death, the king could then claim the land. Ironically, she discovered what she sought in the Hebrew religion and used the laws of God that she had always undermined as an excuse to bring charges against Naboth.

In what ways can we sometimes twist Scripture to suit our own purposes? How can we check ourselves to make sure we don't do this?

Misusing the king's authority, she commanded a call for fasting. This meant that the people would assemble under the assumption of a religious gathering. Fasting in those days meant a humbling of oneself before the holy God[20] who could not leave sin unpunished. In that setting it was easy for Jezebel to set up Naboth as a scapegoat who had released God's wrath. She accused him publicly of having cursed God and the king. Under the laws, anyone who cursed God had to pay the penalty; he had to die.[21]

---

[19] 1 Kings 21:7, author's paraphrase
[20] Psalm 35:13
[21] Leviticus 24:16

Jezebel had organized her plans carefully. In order to make the accusation valid,[22] she made sure that two witnesses were present. Even though they were false witnesses, they did exactly what was expected of them.

Thus Naboth, an innocent man, was stoned to death on Jezebel's orders. His sons shared his fate.[23] King Ahab then added Naboth's land to his possessions.

Jezebel, who had pretended to take the laws of God seriously, undermined them once again. The accusation against Naboth was that he had cursed God and the king. In that way she made the king seem to be as important as God. Again she mocked the living God. Did she think, perhaps, that she had silenced Him forever now that His prophet Elijah seemed to be out of business?

God is not dependent on us to proclaim His name, but He offers us the privilege of doing so. What are specific ways you can proclaim God's name to a dark world?

The moment the king entered Naboth's vineyard to claim it, Elijah suddenly appeared before him. "This is God's message for you," he stated. "Isn't killing Naboth bad enough? Must you rob him too? Because you have done this, dogs shall lick your blood outside the city just as they licked the

22 Deuteronomy 19:15
23 2 Kings 9:26

blood of Naboth,[24] and your descendants shall also die similar deaths."[25] Elijah then prophesied about Jezebel, "Dogs will devour Jezebel by the wall of Jezreel."[26]

The blood of innocent Naboth, his sons, and the prophets of God had not called in vain to God in heaven.[27] Ahab and Jezebel died as predicted.[28]

Jezebel's end, which was particularly terrible, matched her godless rule. Throughout her life, she had continued to be connected with immoral and sorcerous practices.[29] But now God's judgment came swiftly. After being thrown out of a palace window, her body dashed against the ground and was trampled by horses' hooves. Dogs then tore her dead body apart and ate her flesh.

Initially no one noticed Jezebel's corpse. When the decision was later made to bury her—since she had been the daughter and the wife of a king—hardly anything was left of the once proud queen. All the burial party could scrape together were her skull, her feet, and her hands. These body parts were then scattered like manure on a field so that no one could identify them.

God's prophecy about Jezebel had been literally fulfilled. She reaped what she sowed. She sowed on the field of her selfishness and reaped destruction. The words Solomon spoke in the name of God apply to her: "But since you refuse to listen when I call and no one pays attention when I stretch out my

[24] 1 Kings 21:19, author's paraphrase
[25] 1 Kings 21:21, author's paraphrase
[26] 1 Kings 21:2
[27] 2 Kings 9:26
[28] 1 Kings 22:29-40; 2 Kings 9:30-37
[29] 2 Kings 9:22

hand, since you disregard all my advice and do not accept my rebuke, I in turn will laugh when disaster strikes you; I will mock when calamity overtakes you."[30]

God had offered Jezebel many opportunities to turn to Him. As a heathen princess, she had been allowed to live in the land of promise. There she came in contact with His laws and His prophets. She witnessed the great miracles He performed. But she didn't use her opportunities. On the contrary, she mocked the God of Israel and presumptuously committed her evil deeds in the name of religion.

God's love was available to Jezebel, a woman He had created. The many opportunities He gave her to make good use of her life show this. She could have accepted His grace. God had endowed her with an unusual mind. She was keen, intelligent, and resolute. But she had used those capabilities toward exceptionally bad ends. She had willingly and intensely offered them to the service of evil. She had held a high position and could have had a far-reaching and godly influence. But not only did she do what was wrong in the sight of the Lord herself; she also instigated others to do the same.

Consider Jezebel's life in light of Proverbs 1:20-31 and describe the ways in which you think God reached out to her. How might God be reaching out to you right now?

[30] Proverbs 1:24-26

Many centuries later, Jesus lamented about the inhabitants of Israel's capital: "Jerusalem, Jerusalem, you who kill the prophets and stone those sent to you, how often I have longed to gather your children together, as a hen gathers her chicks under her wings, and you were not willing."[31]

Jezebel, likewise, refused to turn to God. She continued to do evil until her death. She proudly believed that she could hold out against God, but that belief turned out to be a painful misconception. No one can trifle with God.

---

[31] Matthew 23:37

11

HERODIAS

A Woman Who Degraded Herself Through Revenge and Murder

When she [a woman] chooses to do good, she blesses more than ever a man can. But the moment she surrenders to sin, her hatred toward the men of God is much more passionate, much fiercer, much more fatal. She will stop at nothing then.

ABRAHAM KUYPER, *WOMEN OF THE NEW TESTAMENT*

READ

Mark 6:17-28

. . .

SALOME, HERODIAS'S DAUGHTER, bent cautiously over to her mother and whispered, "What shall I ask for?"[1]

Herodias could hardly suppress a triumphant smile. Revenge flashed in her eyes. She was not at a loss for an answer, not even for a second.

Have you ever felt the urge for revenge?
If so, what was at the root of those
feelings? If not, what do you think could
cause you to react in such a way?

---

[1] Mark 6:24

"The head of John the Baptist," she hissed.[2] There rang no hesitation in her voice, no trace of doubt. Around her many other people were talking. A select group of people had gathered together in the palace to celebrate the birthday of King Herod Antipas. Many eminent leaders, high military officers, and prominent guests from Galilee had come to the banquet at the ruler's invitation.[3]

Herodias's plan had succeeded. Today she would finally rid herself of the man she hated more intensely than anybody else. Where words had failed, slyness had succeeded. Herod, her husband, would now be forced to kill John. Hadn't he just told Salome in the presence of everyone, "Whatever you ask I will give you"? He had even confirmed those words with: "Up to half my kingdom!"[4]

Herodias knew her husband's inclination toward cruelty. He shared that family streak with his father, Herod the Great.[5] Herod was not a man of high morals. After all, hadn't he repudiated his lawful wife—an Arabian princess—for her, Herodias, the wife of his brother Philip? Hadn't both of them deserted their original life partners in order to live together?

Herodias was also well aware of her husband's pride and sensuality. These traits formed the basis of her speculation and were the reason that she had challenged Salome a few moments earlier to dance before the guests. In this time and

2 Mark 6:24
3 Mark 6:21
4 Mark 6:23
5 Matthew 2:13

surroundings, such dancing was a usual thing to do at a feast, though not for the orthodox Jews.

Pride can be easily manipulated.
In what areas of your life do you struggle
with pride? How can you guard against
sinful responses out of that pride?

The lascivious dance of the girl fascinated the people who had spent the evening eating and drinking. Deciding that this voluntary—and in his eyes fantastic—achievement had to be rewarded highly, the king made his unjustifiable statement.

Herodias also knew that Herod was not a courageous man. He would not dare to acknowledge that he had impulsively promised something he, in fact, didn't really want to deliver. He would not admit that the life of a fellow human being did not belong to the kingdom of an earthly ruler. Although the disposal of a life was not in his hands, in this situation he would not concede that his oath was invalid and of no power.

Proud and egotistical, Herod would choose for his own interests and against those of the prophet. But Herodias had to force that decision on him. Her husband hesitated to harm John of his own accord.

This was not the first time that Herodias had tried to kill John the Baptist. Up to this point her husband had always protected the prophet from her schemes. Every attempt she had made to take John's life had failed. But now she finally had set up a cool and calculating snare for Herod. She had done it so cunningly that her husband was unexpectedly caught in it. The game for the head of John the Baptist was over. Herodias had won.

Her gruesome deed had not sprung from a sudden impulse. She had not acted in an excess of insanity. She had worked on this devilish plan for almost a year and a half. These facts form the background of the ghastly drama that was about to unfold.

The way Herod and Herodias openly lived together mocked the laws of the people among whom they were living. The laws of God condemned what they were doing in very clear words: "If a man marries his brother's wife, it is an act of impurity; he has dishonored his brother. They will be childless."[6]

It was difficult, however, for the subjects of Herod and Herodias to rebuke them. The monarch and his spouse were people of high authority. They represented the Roman emperor whose troops occupied the Jewish country.

But then a man had come who was not deterred by their royal authority. He spoke in the name of God. He, John the Baptist, carried out his orders without respect of persons. His message was strong and simple: "Repent, for the kingdom of heaven has come near."[7]

[6] Leviticus 20:21
[7] Matthew 3:1-6

His voice, in which the roughness and harshness of the desert where he had lived[8] could still be heard, resounded throughout the Jewish land.

The message was not unknown. Earlier prophets, men like Moses[9] and Jeremiah,[10] had extended the same call to conversion. They, too, had exhorted the nation to improve its way of living. If the Israelites would have repented, God would have forgiven their sins and restored their land.[11]

What is something that you are being called to repent of? What has caused you to hesitate?

John's preaching, however, was extremely urgent; the kingdom of heaven was at hand. "Prepare the way for the Lord," he stated. "Make straight paths for him."[12]

Many people recognized the voice of God. They flocked to John in great numbers and confessed their sins. As proof of their changed hearts, they were baptized.

John's voice did not only knock at the doors of his fellow citizens. It also sounded on the gates of the palace of the tetrarch, Herod's proper title.[13] The title of "king," though flattering, was incorrect since he only ruled over the provinces of Galilee and Perea, a quarter of the Jewish land.

Herod and Herodias were not Israelites but Edomites,

---

[8] Luke 1:80
[9] Deuteronomy 30:9-11
[10] Jeremiah 18:11
[11] 2 Chronicles 7:14
[12] Matthew 3:3
[13] Luke 3:19

descendants of Esau. Jacob, from whom the Israelites descended, was not their forefather. They did, however, share the patriarchs Abraham and Isaac with the Israelites. They were distantly related to the Jews among whom they were living.

The message of the prophet was not intended for the Jewish nation alone. It was also intended for Herod and Herodias, for they, too, had to repent. They needed to turn back from the wrong direction in which they were heading. God had a message for them. After their conversion, forgiveness and repair would be available to them.

John was not satisfied to leave them with a general warning. He did not hesitate to warn the couple personally. "It is not lawful for you to have your brother's wife," he told Herod frankly.[14] He also pointed to other crimes that Herod was committing.[15]

A greater difference between the righteous, resolute prophet and the immoral, wavering Herod would hardly be thinkable. Yet a certain relationship had developed between the two men. The king was attracted to the prophet despite the fact that John always told Herod the hard truth. He recognized characteristics in John that he was missing himself: uprightness and a holy way of living. So Herod had summoned John many times in order to listen to him speak. As a result, the king became increasingly confused, but no spiritual changes occurred in his life.

---

[14] Mark 6:18
[15] Luke 3:19-20

---

*What does it mean to be holy? Look back
over your life. How has God grown you in
holiness during your relationship with Him?*

Herodias experienced the yielding of her husband to
the prophet as an additional threat. The woman through
whose influence two marriages had been derailed wanted
to be sure she was not repudiated. From the moment John
exposed their sinful relationship, she hated him—the dis-
turber of her peace. She would get him, somehow!

Herodias wanted to prevent Herod, most of all, from getting further under the influence of the Baptist. So she asked
that John be imprisoned, and finally it was done. The possibility of killing him now seemed to be within her reach, for
the prison was accommodated within the walls of the fort
housing the royal family.

Herod continued to be watchful, however, for his own
sake as well as John's. He knew that John's death could result
in an uproar, for the people unquestionably considered him
to be a prophet.[16] Herod's shaky "throne" might not be able
to outlive such an upheaval.

Thus the prophet who started to bring the people back
to God was locked up in prison. The man of whom Jesus
said, "Among those born of women there has not risen anyone
greater than John the Baptist,"[17] was taken captive. He was

---

[16] Matthew 14:5
[17] Matthew 11:11

the prey of a mean, bloodthirsty woman and a cruel, wavering man. Bereft of his freedom, he sat chained—day after day,
week after week—till he finally doubted his own calling.[18]

Herodias proved her hatred. With deathly precision she
set her snares around John. She also trapped Herod in those
snares by undermining his watchfulness.

Like many parents, Herodias used her child for her own
advantage. Even her daughter was sacrificed to her devilish
scheming, of which the final phase now had arrived.

Salome, influenced by her mother, did not waste any time
bringing her request before the king. Her reactions were even
more heartless than her mother's. Salome realized that her
horrible mission required haste. Her work had to be done
quickly, before the mood of the king changed. Otherwise he
might take back his reckless offer.

"Give me the head of John the Baptist immediately," she
stated cruelly. "And I want it to be presented on a plate."[19]

Even Salome's mother hadn't gone that far. But the hatred
of the mother had poisoned the thoughts of the daughter.
For Salome, it was not enough that John would be murdered
without an open trial, interrogation, or any type of defense.
She was not satisfied that he had to leave this life without saying farewell to his friends. John would continue to be deeply
humiliated after his death; the plate with his stiffened head
supplied the dessert of Herod's birthday party on the explicit
requests of Herodias and Salome.

---

[18] Matthew 11:2-6
[19] Mark 6:25, author's paraphrase

High festive days were opportunities during which monarchs often showed grace, but Herodias horribly degraded this festive day. She murdered an innocent man whose only "crime" was that he spoke the words of God fearlessly, and she made two of her relatives accomplices in her crime.

Christians are being persecuted all over the world for their faith in God. Seek out the story of one or two of those Christians, and commit them to prayer.

Although the names Herod and Herodias meant "heroic," seldom have the meanings of names been such a flagrant contradiction to the life of their bearers. Their deeds did not sprout from heroism. On the contrary, they were dictated by hell.

The portrait gallery of the Bible shows many sinful women, but few of them were as wicked as Herodias. Not many had their hands as stained with blood as she did. The possibility to repent was clearly offered to her, but she rejected it, thus committing her greatest sin.

Before John was taken to prison, he had pointed out a man who traveled in the Jewish land, preaching and doing many miracles—Jesus of Nazareth. "Look, the Lamb of God, who takes away the sin of the world," the Baptist had said.[20] And he added, "I am not of any importance; He is.[21] I am

[20] John 1:29
[21] Mark 1:7, author's paraphrase

only His herald, the voice who announces Him, the finger who points to Him."

The Jews understood this symbolism. Those words foretold that Jesus—like an innocent lamb under their covenant with God[22]—would give His life to redeem them. From now on no more animal sacrifices would be needed to substitute for sinful men. Jesus was the announced Messiah—the Savior of man, of His people, of the entire world.[23]

John exhorted Herod and Herodias so that they might also have a part in this new relationship with God. But to do so, they had to be willing to be humbled. They had to confess their sins, to renew their lives. John wanted them to meet the Messiah who was already living among them. But the couple refused to answer God's call.

How differently the Samaritan woman responded in a similar situation. Like Herodias, she was publically known for her immorality.[24] She also was visited personally, though by Jesus Himself[25] rather than by John.

That woman, realizing that sin had brought her to a blind alley, came to a saving belief. Her life radically changed and became a blessing to others. Other people in her village came to faith in Jesus Christ through her witness.[26]

———————

Study Deuteronomy 30:9-10 and 2 Chronicles 7:14.
What are the requirements for God's blessing?

———————

[22] Exodus 12:1-16
[23] John 3:16
[24] John 4:18
[25] John 4:7-26
[26] John 4:28-39

With Herodias, however, the opposite happened. Her life degenerated. She became a curse to her environment. She had the cruelty to burden the conscience of her own child with the blood of one of God's chosen servants. Salome never showed signs of repentance. Her conscience, like her mother's, was seared beyond recovery.

Herodias also had a destructive influence on her husband. Initially, God had seen an opening with Herod for conversion. The door of his heart had stood ajar for faith till, through Herodias's influence, that door had slammed shut.

When Jesus some time later was sentenced to death, He paid attention to Pilate. At the cross, He even opened heaven for a murderer.[27] But He had nothing to say to Herod.[28] Herod had lost his opportunity. Like Herodias, he had not listened when God spoke to him through John. Both experienced the fact that God often speaks to a person more than once.[29] But when people don't heed His calling, they may lose their chance forever.

Herod, who once had tried to prevent the death of John the Baptist, took an active part in Jesus' death.[30] He continued the murderous tradition of his family. His heart had been hardened.

Herodias's life would have been different if she had corrected herself in time and listened to God's warning. Unfortunately, Herodias preferred sin; she ignored the love of God, who had warned her in time. By refusing to accept

[27] Luke 23:39-43
[28] Luke 23:9
[29] Job 33:14
[30] Luke 23:8-12

the solution to her problem, she invited disaster on herself. She hardened her heart[31] against the teachings of God. Herodias's greatest sin was not adultery or murder; it was unbelief.

"Whoever loves discipline loves knowledge, but whoever hates correction is stupid."[32] Those are the words of Solomon, the wisest man of all time.

"Hold on to instruction, do not let it go," he also cautioned. "Guard it well, for it is your life. . . ."[33] Whoever ignores correction leads others astray."[34]

Herodias rejected the reproof that was meant for her good, and the consequences were disastrous, both materially and spiritually.

Consider a recent reproof from the Lord— whether through His Word or through one of His other children. How did you respond? What did you learn?

Flavius Josephus wrote that Herodias's ambition became her downfall. She overestimated her influence on Herod and incited him to ask Emperor Caligula for the king's title. The request was refused, Herod was exiled, and for the rest of his life he was despised.[35] Herodias shared her husband's

[31] Proverbs 28:14
[32] Proverbs 12:1
[33] Proverbs 4:13
[34] Proverbs 10:17
[35] Flavius Josephus, *Antiquities of the Jews*, Book XVIII, Chapter 7.

humiliation. Such was the reward of a woman who, because of revenge, degraded herself to commit murder.

———————

Are there times in your own life when you fail to listen to God's directions and so miss part of His blessings?

———————

12

SAPPHIRA

A Woman Who Listened to Satan

Voluntary forsaking of property for the sake of the cause of Christ was characteristic of the members of the church at Jerusalem. There has never been, in the long history of the church, such an exhibition of Christian stewardship and a sense of individual responsibility in the sight of God.

HERBERT LOCKYER, *ALL THE WOMEN OF THE BIBLE*

READ

Acts 4:32–5:11

• • •

WHO HAD THE IDEA FIRST, Ananias or Sapphira?

Which one decided to sell a piece of property in order to give the money away to needy people?

It was a marvelous plan, unselfish and sacrificing.

Captivated by a movement that had recently arisen in Jerusalem, Ananias and Sapphira joined a group of people whose dearest desire was to make other people happy. Later these people would be called Christians,[1] named after their Savior and great example, Jesus Christ.

---

[1] Acts 11:26

In Jerusalem, something special had happened. Ten days after the ascension of Jesus, the Holy Spirit had descended on His followers exactly as predicted. That Spirit had captivated the hearts of the believers, changing them radically. A mutual bond of love and unity grew among them such as no one had ever thought possible. They experienced a relationship that had never before existed and that afterward was largely forgotten.

What differences do you see between the early church and the church of today? Why do you think those differences exist?

The believers met daily with one another in the temple. They wanted to be together. They sought out one another and ate their meals together. God was central in their thoughts and conversations.

What role does God play in the conversations and interactions you have with your Christian friends? Does He permeate the atmosphere of those relationships, or does He play a minor role? Why do you think that is?

In such situations, social differences can be painful. How can one enjoy his possessions when other people have deep needs? The Spirit of Jesus had come to live within them. It was His compassion that they experienced. Like Him, they wanted to serve others, to make other people happy. From that point on they wanted to be good stewards of their possessions. Without anyone urging them to do so, the rich sold their possessions. The proceeds were then placed in a mutual fund from which everyone received a share as needed.

The first church of Jesus Christ was inwardly united through faith in Him. Its members were also equal in their outward circumstances, because the privileged members gave of their possessions in favor of the needy.

Joseph, also called Barnabas, was a particularly striking man among them. His name meant "son of encouragement," and that is exactly what he was. He sold the field he owned and brought the money to the apostles. Everyone began to talk about this man and the good example he had set.

Since the church was thinking spiritually, its members were convinced of the relative and temporal value of earthly possessions. Had not the Master said with much emphasis that unless a person renounced all he had, he could not be His disciple?[2]

Since their thoughts were first of all concerned with the things of the kingdom of God, the Christians were convinced that God would take care of them.[3] Hadn't Jesus assured that those who gave up relatives, homes, or property for Him and the gospel would receive back one hundred times over?[4]

[2] Luke 14:33
[3] Matthew 6:33
[4] Mark 10:29-30

*How do you view financial giving in
the church? What are your motivations
for giving or not giving?*

No wonder that the believers who were living according
to these godly standards were popular with all of the people.
Every day people who believed in Jesus Christ, the resur-
rected One, were being added to the church.[5]

In those days, many mighty miracles were happening that
filled everyone with awe, including Ananias and Sapphira.
Under no other pressure than that of their own consciences,
this couple decided voluntarily to follow the examples they
saw around them. They didn't want to fall behind Barnabas
and the others. Their splendid decision to sell a piece of land
and give the earnings away was mutual.

Satan had viewed the developments of the first Christians
with hatred. He was looking for ways to curtail their growth and
happiness. Because every person who joined the church was a
loss for his kingdom,[6] he could not remain inactive.

Satan looked into the hearts of Ananias and Sapphira and
discovered that their faith was not of the same quality as that
of Barnabas. He discovered that they had a double motive.
They wanted to do good, on the one hand, and sought to
make an impression on the other.

[5] Acts 2:43-47
[6] Acts 26:18

*Have you ever done something good out of
a selfish motivation? What was the result?*

Ananias and Sapphira were not only concerned about the poor. They also desired to gain honor and admiration for themselves. Their aim was in part unspiritual. They wanted to show themselves better than they were. Maybe fear had also crept in after their initial decision. Now that they were older, they were less cared for and the future was uncertain.

Whatever their reasons, they agreed to keep part of the money from the property they had sold for themselves, while pretending that they gave it all. Otherwise people would not think as highly of them as they did of Barnabas. Fully aware of their well-thought-through decision, Ananias and Sapphira carried out their plan at the cost of their lives.

When Peter accepted the money from Ananias, he knew that deceit was being practiced. His terrifying greeting was, "Ananias, how is it that Satan has so filled your heart that you have lied to the Holy Spirit and have kept for yourself some of the money you received for the land?"[7]

Peter's words disclosed the extent and the seriousness of the deception. Ananias had allowed Satan to occupy his heart. Like the first couple on earth, Adam and Eve, he and Sapphira had surrendered themselves to be deceived by Satan.[8] As always, Satan was aiming to destroy the work of God.

[7] Acts 5:3
[8] Genesis 3:1-8

Peter knew that deceiving the Holy Spirit was deceiving God. "The property was yours to sell or not, as you wished. And after selling it, it was yours to decide how much to give," Peter continued. "How could you do a thing like this? You weren't lying to us, but to God!"[9]

With those words Ananias dropped dead. He was not condemned because his gift was not large enough, but because it was connected with dishonesty. His good deed came to nothing because of his double-heartedness and lying. He had, first of all, failed God, and then tried to dupe the needy. His decision put God's holiness in the balance and dishonored Him through deceit. That cost him his life.

---

*Have you ever tried to lie to God? If not,
what do you think that might look like?
What do you learn from this passage?*

The God whom Ananias and Sapphira had largely ignored is a holy God. He "is a consuming fire."[10] No creature is hidden before Him, but all are open and laid bare to His eyes.[11] This was also true of the thoughts of Ananias and Sapphira. They, too, had to give account of their deeds to God, and who could exist when He administered justice instead of mercy?

Petrified, the people who were present watched as the

---

[9] Acts 5:4, author's paraphrase
[10] Hebrews 12:29
[11] Hebrews 4:13

younger men covered Ananias's body with a sheet and immediately carried him away to be buried.

Jerusalem was small. From any point in the city, it was a short walk to the temple square. When her husband still had not returned home after about three hours, Sapphira went out to investigate. When she entered the room to speak with Peter and the apostles, they were still thinking about the terrible thing that had happened. In the distance sounded the footsteps of the young men returning from Ananias's burial.

Did Sapphira sense the tension filling the room? Is that the reason that she didn't dare to ask where her husband was?

Nobody told her what had happened. She would also have to stand the test her husband had taken and failed.

Peter took up the thread of conversation with Sapphira as if no time had passed since the death of Ananias. "Tell me, is this the price you and Ananias got for the land?"[12]

God was giving Sapphira a second opportunity. She had missed the first one—the chance to respond with her husband in an honest way toward God and His followers.

But Sapphira also showed herself to be in the power of Satan. So her answer was forcibly short and without hesitation. "Yes . . . that is the price."[13]

"How could you and your husband even think of doing a thing like this, conspiring together to test the Spirit of God?" Peter lashed out at her.[14]

The terrifying fact of the sin of Ananias and Sapphira was

---

[12] Acts 5:8
[13] Acts 5:8
[14] Acts 5:9, author's paraphrase

that it was premeditated. They were fully aware of what they were doing. Sin had not taken them by surprise; they played with it deliberately. For her sin, Sapphira also died.

What safeguards can you take to avoid the path that leads to deliberate sin?

Meanwhile the young men returned to the house. They were just in time to bury Sapphira.

Sapphira made an impression, indeed. But it was not a positive one. She left behind memories of fear, fright, and dismay with both the Christians and all those outside the church who heard about the cause of her death.

Sapphira's name meant "sapphire," but the only sparkle she was able to give was that of a grim warning.

About the Author

GIEN KARSSEN was raised in a Christian home and became a Christian at the age of twelve as a result of the influence of her parents' lives and training. After she had been married only six weeks, the Nazis interned her husband in a concentration camp, where he died. Just before his death, he inscribed Luke 9:62 in his diary: "But Jesus said to him, 'No one, after putting his hand to the plow and looking back, is fit for the kingdom of God'" (NASB). This verse challenged Gien and gave purpose and direction to her life. Using this Scripture as a basis, she found it easier to face difficulties, cancel her own desires, and want God's will only.

She met Dawson Trotman, founder of The Navigators, in 1948 in Doorn, Holland. She started the Navigator ministry there by translating The Navigators' *Topical Memory System* into Dutch and handling all the enrollments. Over the years she worked in many capacities with The Navigators. Women who have been personally helped by Gien Karssen can be found on almost every continent of the globe.

Gien was a popular speaker, Bible study leader, and trainer, as well as a freelance writer for Christian periodicals in Europe. The original edition of *Her Name Is Woman* (Book 1) was her first book and the first book ever published by NavPress. She also wrote *Beside Still Waters* and *The Man Who Was Different*.

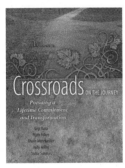

Become the Woman God Created You to Be.

Becoming a Woman of Simplicity
978-1-60006-663-4 | DVD 978-1-61521-821-9

What does it mean to enter into God's rest? Can women today do that, with multitasking, constant communication, and others clamoring for attention? Bestselling author Cynthia Heald helps you quiet the chaos and find true rest for your soul.

Becoming a Woman of Grace
978-1-61521-022-0

This inspirational study guides you on a life-transforming journey into the boundless riches of God's grace. You will explore the many ways in which God's grace enriches your Christian walk and discover how to know His grace more fully.

Becoming a Woman Who Loves
978-1-61521-023-7

In *Becoming a Woman Who Loves*, you'll explore the incredible nature of Christlike love and how God empowers us to love as Jesus loved.

Becoming a Woman of Faith
978-1-61521-021-3

This book will strengthen and encourage you as Cynthia shares candidly from her own faith journey. You'll see yourself in her personal struggles to walk in faith and trust, and you'll learn and grow from her special insights from God's Word.

Becoming a Woman of Strength
978-1-61521-620-8 | DVD 978-1-61747-902-1

We constantly encounter struggles and hardships of all kinds in our lives, but we can respond to them in our own weakness or with God's strength. This Bible study will encourage you to depend upon the strength of the Lord by seeking, waiting, serving, praying, and persevering in Him.

Available wherever books are sold.

NAVPRESS

A NavPress resource published in alliance
with Tyndale House Publishers, Inc.   CP0794

Becoming a Woman of Excellence
978-1-57683-832-7

Society beckons us to succeed — to achieve excellence in our appearance, our earning power, our family life. God Himself also beckons us to be women of excellence. But what exactly is He asking? In this motivational Bible study, you will discover what you should be striving for as you look to God's excellence as a model.

Becoming a Woman of Freedom
978-1-57683-829-7

Is your Christian life weighing you down? Get your second wind to identify and lay aside those burdens that make you feel "stuck." With challenging insights and thought-provoking quotations from classic thinkers and writers, *Becoming a Woman of Freedom* will help you develop the actions and attitudes you need to finish the race with strength.

Becoming a Woman of Prayer
978-1-57683-830-3

In *Becoming a Woman of Prayer*, you will be encouraged to respond to God's invitation to deeper intimacy with Him. Prayer is an opportunity for us to respond to His invitation to intimacy by calling, crying, and singing to Him. This guide shows us how to become women of prayer.

Becoming a Woman of Purpose
978-1-57683-831-0

As you grow toward genuine peace and fulfillment, you'll learn the joy of loving God and others, waiting on Him with hope, trusting Him through suffering, serving Him with reverent fear, and fulfilling His purposes.

Becoming a Woman Whose God Is Enough
978-1-61291-634-7

God desires to bless you with His fullness and to teach you to depend on Him completely. Learn to turn from worldly satisfactions to a life of contentment, from selfishness to humility, and from unbelief to rich fellowship with God.

Available wherever books are sold.

A NavPress resource published in alliance with Tyndale House Publishers, Inc.   CP0795

Women of the Bible You Can Relate To

Believers

Jochebed	Elizabeth
Hannah	Anna
Rahab	The Poor Widow
The Jewish Maid	Mary of Jerusalem
Ruth	Tabitha
Mary	Lois and Eunice

Leaders

Miriam	Esther
Deborah	Mary of Bethany
Abigail	Mary Magdalene
The Queen of Sheba	Lydia
Huldah	Priscilla
The Shunammite	Phoebe

Learners

Eve	Naomi
Sarah	Bathsheba
Rebekah	The Widow of Zarephath
Leah	Martha of Bethany
Dinah	The Samaritan Woman
Tamar	Salome

Wanderers

Hagar	Job's Wife
Lot's Wife	Orpah
Rachel	Michal
Potiphar's Wife	Jezebel
Delilah	Herodias
Peninnah	Sapphira

Gien Karssen's vivid storytelling and deep insights will immerse you in the lives of these women. As you grapple with God's role in each woman's life, you will be inspired to live your own life wholeheartedly for God.

The Her Name Is Woman series is a favorite guide for Bible studies and small groups, with relevant Scripture passages and Bible study questions.

Available everywhere books are sold or online at NavPress.com.
1-855-277-9400

CP0927